W9-BEU-880

LEARN WITH THE *CLASSICS*

Using Music to Study Smart at Any Age

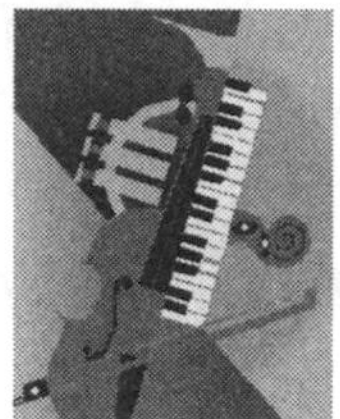

Powerful Learning Skills
for Students,
Teachers,
and Parents

LIND®
Institute

Copyright 1999 by the LIND Institute

The cover and content of ***Learn with the Classics*** are fully protected by copyright and cannot be reproduced in any manner without prior written permission, except in the form of brief excerpts or quotations with acknowledgment of the source. All rights reserved in all countries.

Learn with the Classics, ***Active Relaxation***, and ***Beautiful Music That's Good for You*** are trademarks of the LIND Institute.

First Edition

ISBN: 1-883095-01-8

Printed in the United States of America
Book design by *Design/communications* (Ross, CA) and *Jeoflin D. Roh* (San Francisco, CA)

LIND®
Institute
P.O. Box 14487 • San Francisco, CA 94114 • From overseas, call 415-864-3396
Fax: 415-864-1742 • E-Mail: lind@lind-institute.com
1-800-LEARN-R-US
(1-800-532-7678)
Visit our web site at: www.lind-institute.com

CONTENTS

How to Get Started with *Learn with the Classics*

What will you get out of *Learn with the Classics?*

As you use the book and the music, you'll find the answers to these questions:

- Why should I use music for learning and studying?
- How do I use music?
- What music should I use?
- What do I do if I don't like classical music?
- How can this music make me feel better?
- How can using music make studying and learning more fun?
- How does music affect my memory?
- How will using music make me more creative?
- How will using music reduce stress and fear?
- How exactly do I use the music while I study? (before, during, and after)

How do you use *Learn with the Classics?*

Learn with the Classics is made up of several components that will guide you in finding the information that is of interest to you. Begin by scanning through ***Learn with the Classics***, using the following elements to familiarize yourself with its contents:

Highlights

At the beginning of each section, several particularly useful and interesting section topics

Preview

Summary of key information that you'll learn in each section

Study Tips

Easy-to-implement learning techniques for quickly getting more "bang for your buck" from your studying

Learning Strategies

A blueprint for your own successful studying and learning plan

Review

A bulleted bare-bones summary of all the key info from each section

Reflection

A topic to contemplate after each section, helping you become comfortable with and remember what you've learned

From Learning to Doing

At the end of each section, suggestions for using what you've just learned, which lets you plant the information in your memory, which then makes it active rather than passive and enables you to own it

Two Types of *From Learning to Doing*

Let's Go

For those who like to get going with what they've learned and start using it right away, fun activities to experiment with as soon as you've finished each section

Show Me

For those not yet convinced of the value of the information they've been given so far, suggestions for familiarizing yourself with the material at your own pace

Resources and References

After each section, a guide to books, products, organizations, and so forth, where you can get additional information

Sidebars

Information of special interest—not absolutely necessary to read, but quite useful, especially to those who have curiosity about the topic

Let Music Prime Your Brain for Learning

SECTION 1

HIGHLIGHTS

- How Music Primes Your Brain for Learning
- Health and Learning: The Sound Connection
- Factual Thinking, Creative Thinking: You Need Them Both
- Baroque Music—Balanced and Complete

Your Magnificent and Powerful Brain

Preview

In this section, you will learn how important it is to prime your powerful brain for learning; you'll learn how to accomplish this with music; and you'll begin doing it yourself.

Your brain affects everything you do in both your body and your mind. Of course, you know that already, but if you're like most people on the planet, you take it for granted. Your brain works so well all by itself that it isn't necessary for you to be bothered about knowing what it's doing.

With *Learn with the Classics*, you will learn to use music to prime your brain for learning and studying, which will make these activities much less stressful and much more fun.

By really understanding and experiencing the powerful effects that certain music has on your brain and your body, however, you can prompt your brain to do so much more for you, an amazing amount more. With ***Learn with the Classics***, you will learn to use music to prime your brain for learning and studying, which will make these activities much less stressful and much more fun. Using the music will also help you memorize information more easily.

Music with the Right Stuff

The pieces on ***Learn with the Classics,*** the recording that comes with this book, have been selected and the format has been structured to prime your brain to function at its best with no extra effort on your part, which maximizes your learning potential and assists you in getting the most out of your studying time. The greatest portion of the music is from the *Baroque* period in history, discussed more later on. ***Learn with the Classics, The Recording,*** is a sampler of musical selections from a series of classical recordings, ***Relax with the Classics.*** The series was designed specifically to enhance learning. It is used worldwide by corporate trainers, universities, educators at all levels, and well-informed students who are aware of the power of this kind of music in learning and studying. But we invite you to find out for yourself—firsthand. ***Learn with the Classics*** is an interactive experience.

The music on this recording automatically relaxes you. It has a consistent beat of 55–70 beats per minute, your pulse rate at rest. When you are too tense to study or learn, as you listen to the music for even a short time, your pulse rate will automatically slow down to mirror the beat of the music. In addition, the music will cause the blood vessels in your brain to stop contracting (which they do when you're under stress). This allows more blood to flow through your brain, making you more alert and ready to learn.

> ***Select music with the characteristics needed to power up your studying.***
>
> 55–70-beats-per-minute Baroque music slows down your pulse to mirror the beat of the music; it focuses you; and it makes you more alert and ready to learn.

In general, for the purpose of studying, it is beneficial to play music that is not so attention grabbing as to totally occupy your attention. For the same reason, you may want to keep the volume low, so the music doesn't distract you. It's important only that *your brain hears the music.* It is neither necessary nor desirable for you to be keenly aware of each note that is playing. Occasionally, however, you will probably find it relaxing and effective to allow yourself to listen attentively to or "get carried away by" a particularly pleasurable part of the music and then return to your work. Be aware that when you are pulled in by the music, it means that the piece is special to you, that it uplifts you, that it makes you feel good. Stay with it for a minute or two before returning to your studying.

Reflection—An Easy-to-Do Technique That Pays off Big Time

It is especially important—for getting the most out of each studying and learning experience—that you take time out to reflect on what you've just learned. It only takes a few minutes, but it's worth hours of study time if you develop the habit of allowing your mind the time to drift and relax after you've studied for a while. When you've finished a studying session (or during periodic breaks while you're studying), put down your work and relax your mind and body. Let your mind contemplate what you've just been learning, with no structured thinking, no concerns, just a kick-back-and-relax brief period of reflection, during which a connection is made between what you have just learned and what you already know. This connection is necessary for storing information in your memory. You can close your eyes if you like, put your feet up, lean back, however you're most comfortable. Generally, for reflection, turn the volume up a bit, so the music will pull you in and relax you.

LEARNING 2 STRATEGY

Reflect on what you've learned after each studying session.

This means relaxing completely and letting your brain and the music do the work for you.

There's no right way or wrong way to play this music, either while you study or while you relax and reflect on what you've learned.

Play around with the volume settings over the next few days. You'll soon discover the best levels for you while you're studying and while you're reflecting. This music is yours to use. It's here to assist you.

Let's Get Started

So, let's begin. Put on ***Learn with the Classics, The Recording***, so you can start having a great learning and listening experience right now, as you read on.

As you now listen to the music, it is beginning to have a very positive effect on your brain and your body. This is happening spontaneously—whether you are aware of it or not. What the music is doing for you is automatic. Your brain is being primed to learn efficiently and effectively. The music is relaxing your body and creating an optimal learning environment.

The first piece on the recording, which you are hearing right now, is called *Air on G String*. It was written by Johann Sebastian Bach in the eighteenth century. It remains one of the most beloved compositions of all time. This is for several reasons, one of which is how melodic it is; you can easily hum along with it. For centuries, people have been attracted to its beauty. Another reason, though, is the relaxation effect that the rhythm has on the listener. Because of both the slow tempo and the musical structure, it is now automatically altering your brain patterns, making them more efficient. You are getting primed to learn, as your brain and body are synchronizing with the music.

How Does Music Prime Your Brain for Learning? By Enabling You to Change Brain Wave States

Throughout each day, you function in four brain wave states: *beta*, *alpha*, *theta*, and *delta*. Beta is a high-speed state. Most of the time, during your daily activities, your brain is in beta. It's the "doing" state, which gives you the energy to go about your business and get things done. The alpha state is slower and more relaxed. It's the reflecting state, which gives you access to your most creative ideas and insights. It allows you to imagine, to invent, to originate. Theta is the dreamlike state you're in just before you drift into sleep or if you're in very deep contemplation or meditation. Delta is the state of sleep itself. In both theta and delta, you have no sense of time. You're completely suspended in the experiences you're having.

Beta and alpha are the states you operate in during your waking day. When you first put on the recording, your brain was in beta. It was active. If you continue to listen to the music at a very noticeable volume level, your brain will shift to alpha. It will then become reflective. In most instances, when you are studying—reading, taking notes, organizing material, and so forth—you will have the music on very low, so your brain will stay in the "doing" state of beta, the thinking state. When used in this way, the Baroque music functions to focus your attention on your studies and keep you focused. When you take breaks for reflection, turn the music up and become more attentive to it. You will shift to your creative alpha state. It is the music's ability to shift your brain between alpha and beta that primes your brain for learning.

Music, Active Relaxation, and Sound Learning

As you listen to the music now, your *autonomic nervous system* is slowing down, which is healthful for your body. The autonomic nervous system is the "automatic pilot" portion of your nervous system. The music is not only readying your brain for learning but also making your body healthier. A healthy body is just as important for first-rate learning as a primed brain. Moving toward this healthy state, your mind is becoming both more relaxed *and* more alert. (Yes, both at the same time!) We call this ideal learning and studying state *active relaxation*. In this state, you are most ready to learn at your best. As a matter of fact, you're learning very easily right now!

Great Health and Great Learning: The Sound Connection

Because the same conditions that make you physically healthy also heighten your learning potential, it has been frequently reported that when people learn through *Accelerated Learning* (a sophisticated and powerful learning technique that uses this kind of music), they experience noticeable improvements in their physical health. Be alert to that. After using ***Learn with the Classics*** for a few days, you will likely become aware of increased feelings of well-being and optimism. Start paying attention to these feelings. Stressful events will not bother you as much. As a matter of fact, whenever you feel stressed out or uncomfortably wired, listen to ***Learn with the Classics***. Your body and mind *will* calm down, and you *will* feel much better.

Baroque music is a joy to listen to for most people of all heritages and cultures, but it's not even important that you like the music to get great results. The music is for your brain, not your taste!

A case in point: As Don Campbell notes in his book *The Mozart Effect*, "In Washington State, Immigration Department officials play Mozart and Baroque music during English classes for new arrivals from Cambodia, Laos, and other Asian countries and report that it speeds up their learning." Obviously, people from Eastern cultures have little if any exposure to seventeenth- and eighteenth-century European music! But it works anyway.

If you study in an environment that is noisy, you will notice that the music masks that distracting noise. Pay attention to the difference this makes in your ability to focus on your studies and to feel greater relaxation during these study periods.

Shift Effortlessly Between Brain Wave States and Get Your Learning in Gear

Your brain must shift back and forth between alpha and beta for you to get the most out of any studying and learning experience. The most creative and productive people constantly shift back and forth between the relaxed, reflective, kind of daydreaming alpha state (the domain of feelings and insights and art) and the active, rational, sensible beta state (the domain of organizing information and getting things done). For this reason, it is important to have regular periods of daydreaming or some form of relaxed contemplation during your learning and studying activities. So, to learn and create, you need to have access to both alpha and beta states.

Good scholars in the sciences frequently operate for extended periods in the alpha state.

Everyone knows that you have to be able to think, to organize, and to structure information—all beta stuff. But you also need to reflect, to calm your thinking mind, to imagine—all alpha stuff. Right now, you are gaining access to the most foolproof method of shifting effortlessly between alpha and beta—this slow Baroque music. Over time and with consistent use, this tool will aid you in comprehending material, remembering information, and applying it with skill and confidence.

How Do You Get into Alpha?

Let's say you're studying a mathematical or a philosophical theory, or maybe you're reading some historical narrative. *It is very effective to take a few seconds to integrate the new information with what you already know*. By stopping your studying for a little while and using the music as a trigger, you will shift your brain into a reflective state. Then you're operating in alpha. In this state, you can easily link the information you have just learned to information that you already know. The alpha state—accessed through the music—provides the condition you need to make connections between newly learned information and what exists in your long-term memory. To transfer information in the brain from your short-term memory to your long-term memory and to do so efficiently, you need to experience some extended periods of alpha learning.

Factual Thinking, Creative Thinking: You Need Them Both

Good scholars in the sciences frequently operate for extended periods in alpha. First, they'll be very intense in beta (factual thinking). Then they'll shift to a period of reflection (creative thinking). It's during these reflective states that they get their insights. Then they come back to attentiveness—to beta, to productivity. Einstein is a great example of a first-rate reflective thinker. Most creative writers and painters function this way as well. For you to develop the kind of advanced intellectual activity that you will need to succeed in any field of study or creativity, you must experience these shifts between alpha and beta states frequently.

The music does the work for you. Your body and brain respond automatically. It's a win-win for you.

Shift between alpha and beta brain wave states at will.

As you become familiar with using the music, you will become skilled at shifting states depending upon what kind of thinking you want to engage in at the time—factual or creative.

Baroque Music—Balanced and Complete

The music you're listening to now is from the Baroque period, which was from about 1600–1750. Johann Sebastian Bach (1685–1750), a German composer whom many, maybe most, music scholars consider to be the finest Baroque composer, intuitively knew about balancing alpha and beta states, though there were no such concepts back then. (It's interesting to note that the Baroque period ended with Bach's death. The consensus of opinion among music scholars is that after Bach died, there was no one left who could write in that complex and artful style as well as he could.) Another German composer, Georg-Friedrich Handel (1685–1759), and an Italian composer, Antonio Vivaldi (1678–1741), two other great Baroque masters, also wrote music that causes shifts between the two brain wave states. Some sections in their music are very intense and dramatic and then suddenly change, becoming very slow and calm. This is why you feel so complete after listening to their compositions.

For the purposes of studying and learning, only slow Baroque movements (55–70 beats per minute) were chosen for the ***Relax with the Classics*** series. (See the section on Baroque music, starting on p. 44.)

Study Tip

Take a reflection break about every 15 minutes to contemplate what you've been studying and to allow the information to enter your long-term memory. Keep the music playing. Turn it up a bit so you can hear it a little better.

Live with the Music and Discover Its Powerful Effects

We invite you simply to live with the music over the next few days. Whenever it's appropriate for you, play it and just experience it, with no expectations. Play it not only while you study but also while you work, or while you drive, or while you kick back and relax. Simply be with the music. Observe it and observe yourself and your own feelings.

All of the selections on the ***Relax with the Classics*** recordings were chosen after listening to thousands of pieces of music. These pieces have been selected, in part, because you can listen to them over and over again, without ever getting tired of hearing them.

Review and Reflection

Review

Key points you've learned in Section 1:

1. What are my four brain-wave states?

- Beta—high-speed state, for active doing (factual thinking)
- Alpha—slower state, for relaxing and reflecting (creative thinking)
- Theta—dreamlike state, for drifting off outside of time
- Delta—sleeping state, for total resting of body and brain

2. Why is it important for me to go into alpha when I'm learning and studying?

- To slow down your autonomic nervous system, which is healthful for the body
- To prime your brain for creativity
- To enable you to store information in your long-term memory

3. Why do I need to shift back and forth between alpha and beta to learn at my best?

- Alpha state accesses your unique creativity, insight, and originality.
- Beta state accesses your rational thinking, and your organizational and structural skills.
- Both states are needed to achieve complete and full learning.

4. How can I use the music to help me shift back and forth between alpha and beta?

- Play it when you're studying (at a lower, undistracting volume) to support your learning and stay focused.
- Play it when you're reflecting on what you've studied (at a slightly louder, more noticeable volume) to remember what you've learned.

5. Who are the three Baroque composers I've read about in this section?

- Johann Sebastian Bach (1685–1750), a German composer

- Georg-Friedrich Handel (1685–1759), a German composer
- Antonio Vivaldi (1678–1741), an Italian composer

6. When was the Baroque period in history? What famous composer's death signaled the end of the era?

- The Baroque period was from 1600–1750.
- The Baroque period ended with the death of J. S. Bach.

Reflection

Turn up the volume on the music a little to influence your thoughts and shift your brain into alpha. We invite you to reflect on the brain wave states you have moved through while reading this section. Guess at which point you may have been in alpha and when you may have been in beta. Let your mind wander. Whatever you reflect on is interesting and useful.

From Learning to Doing

For you to be confident that you have learned the material that you've been taught or that you've been studying, you need the material to be *activated,* which means it *has to be used* within a day after you have learned it. This section, *From Learning to Doing,* suggests ways for you to activate the information you're learning. As you take part in these activations, you'll be learning how to activate information in your own studies. In essence, your practicing this technique will serve as a prototype that you can apply to all of your learning experiences.

From Learning to Doing is separated into two parts: *Let's Go* and *Show Me. Let's Go* is for those who like to get going with what they've learned and start using it right away. *Let's Go* offers fun activities that you can experiment with as soon as you've finished each section. *Show Me* is for those not yet convinced of the value of the information they've been given so far. *Show Me* offers suggestions for familiarizing yourself with the material at your own pace.

Let's Go

There's no time like the present to start making use of the information in ***Learn with***

continued next page . . .

Show Me

Many people, those who tend to be analytical (like so many scientists and lawyers,

continued next page . . .

Let's Go . . . continued . . .

the Classics. If you're ready to roll, jump in right now. You will be taking the first steps toward designing your own personalized, step-by-step study plan, which you can apply to your own subjects. Your study plan will include music, reflections, the learning strategies and study tips that you've read about in *Section 1,* plus all the other powerful techniques you'll discover as you go along.

Think of a subject you are currently studying, one that presents a special challenge to you. Perhaps you find the material complex or perplexing. Perhaps you find it boring or believe it isn't being taught effectively. Start using the techniques and tools you are discovering in ***Learn with the Classics*** to design a study plan for this subject. Start with the following:

1. Select music that is 55–70 beats per minute and that has the other characteristics mentioned in this section, and play it as you study. Experiment with lowering and raising the volume, basing your choice on the brain wave state—alpha or beta—that you want to enter at a given time. The recording that comes with ***Learn with the Classics*** meets all these criteria and would certainly be a great way to start. Later, when you become more skilled, you can experiment with other music that meets these specifications.

continued next page . . .

Show Me . . . continued . . .

for example), require a substantial amount of information or scientific proof to be "convinced" of the value of something. Each of us needs a different amount of information before we feel comfortable trying out new things. The more information that a person needs to be convinced, the more that individual is a *Show Me* person. It helps to understand that about ourselves, to be aware of our requirements, so we can work with them and not be ruled by them. See *Section 2* for more information on the requirements of a *Show Me* person.

If you are not yet convinced of the value or effectiveness of the information you have been given so far, you may need to read on and sample the material in the sections to come before you decide to activate what you have learned here. In the meantime, just be with the music in the days ahead, get to know it, and enjoy it with no expectations.

For now, get a sense of how the information you have just learned (and which may have become a permanent part of your brain's information library) may affect your future study. Reflect on this.

Whenever you are ready, experiment with the activations suggested in *Let's Go.*

Let's Go . . . continued . . .

2. Plan for short reflection breaks (under 5 minutes) after every 15 minutes of studying and for longer reflection breaks (10 to 15 minutes) after every 45 minutes of studying. Pay attention to this schedule, and see if it is effective for you. Adjust the timing of breaks over the next few weeks and months to suit your own needs and preferences.

3. Start getting accustomed to and comfortable with the alpha brain wave state during your reflections. Pay attention to how you feel when you stop to reflect and listen to the music. You'll begin to see how easy it is to shift between factual and creative thinking at will. In the days and weeks ahead, begin to notice the feeling of calmness that you experience after listening to the music. Notice how your thoughts wander in new directions, how you see your surroundings in a different light, and how you begin to get new ideas and insights. It's a new kind of experience, and it's fun and effective.

4. Start paying attention whenever you get a sense that you are connecting new information with something you already know. As you begin to notice this happening, you'll see how this process really anchors information more firmly in your long-term memory. You'll begin to have confidence that you are definitely learning what you want to learn.

Resources and References

For information on music for learning:

LIND Institute
P.O. Box 14487, San Francisco, CA 94114
1-800-LEARN-R-US (1-800-532-7678)
From overseas: 415-864-3396
FAX: 415-864-1742, E-Mail: lind@lind-institute.com
Visit our web site at: www.lind-institute.com

LIND produces the series **Relax with the Classics,** *Baroque and classical music scientifically selected and sequenced to be used for learning and studying.* *See page 93 for information about these educational products.*

For information on Accelerated Learning:

> **Accelerated Learning Systems** (ALS)
> 800 Grand Ave., Suite A14, Carlsbad, CA 92008
> 760-434-7070, web site: www.accelerated-learning.com

ALS offers Accelerated Learning for the 21st Century, *a book by Colin Rose and Malcolm Nicholl, as well as Accelerated Learning foreign language courses on tape.*

> **International Alliance for Learning** (IAL)
> 1040 First St., Encinitas, CA 92024
> 1-800-426-2989, From overseas: 619-634-5146

IAL is an international organization for teachers, trainers, educators, and anyone interested in Accelerated Learning. They offer an annual three-day conference in January in a different U.S. city each year and can provide information on trainers and companies involved in Accelerated Learning.

> **Superlearning Inc.**
> 450 Seventh Avenue, Suite 500, New York, NY 10123
> 212-279-8450, web site: www.Superlearning.com

Superlearning Inc. offers the books, Superlearning *and* Superlearning 2000, *by Sheila Ostrander, Lynn Schroeder, and Nancy Ostrander..*

Campbell, D. *The Mozart Effect.* New York: Avon Books, 1997.

Harvey, A. "Accessing the Whole Brain with Music in the Classroom." *Consortium for Whole Brain Learning,* Feb. 1988, *3* (3).

Harvey, A. "An Intelligence View of Music Education." *Hawaii Music Educators' Association Bulletin,* Feb. 1997, *97* (1), 15–18.

Miles, E. *Tune Your Brain: Using Music to Manage Your Mind, Body, and Mood.* New York: Berkley, 1997.

Study Smart

SECTION 2

How Do You Know if You Have Learned Something?

Preview

In this section, you will learn how to use some highly effective studying techniques, which have been devised by experts and proven by research to power up your learning capacity.

HIGHLIGHTS

- Know What Is in Your Memory and What Isn't
- How You Feel Determines How Well You Do
- Learning by Doing Is As Vital As Learning by Seeing and Hearing

Oftentimes, students who are trying hard to be diligent and to learn everything they need for a test will underline or highlight too many things in their textbooks. Sometimes, practically the whole page is highlighted! This is counterproductive. When you go back to review for your test, you have to read practically the whole book. Again! This is not useful, even though the intentions are really good. Here is a study technique on how to prepare for tests:

Study Tip

What should I do when I come across important information in the text I'm studying?

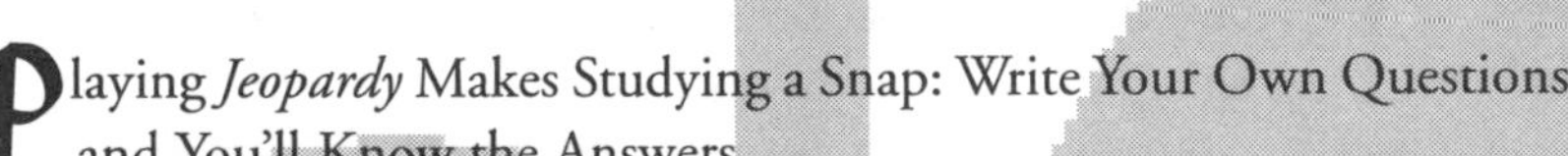

Playing *Jeopardy* Makes Studying a Snap: Write Your Own Questions and You'll Know the Answers.

A major university study revealed that a very simple, efficient, and time-saving study technique is an almost foolproof way to pass tests! Just as in the popular and fun game show *Jeopardy* (in which the contestants come up with the questions to the answers they're given), coming up with your own questions will ultimately give you the right answers.

The technique is simple: When initially reading your material, whenever you come to a specific piece of information, write a question in the margin so that the answer to the question is that piece of information. (If the textbook belongs to the school, don't write in the book. Use Post-its and place them in the margins.) Do this consistently as you go through

continued next page . . .

Study Tip

Study Tip . . . continued . . .

the text. It's important to do it every time you come to a fact or a series of facts that the author is stressing.

How do I use the questions I've written in the margin to study for a test?

When you review for your test, go back and read your questions. Whenever you can answer a question, great! Just keep on going. You obviously know the answer. When you come to a question that you cannot answer, reread only the portion of text that has the answer. Once you can answer all of your own questions, you have studied sufficiently. You'll be amazed at how much you already know, so that there is no need to reread a great deal of the material. This way, you can efficiently focus your studying only on what you still need to learn.

In general, what percentage of questions that I've written will be on the actual test?

Here's the kicker: The study showed that 70% of the questions asked in tests are the same questions that you have come up with, so on average, you will have already passed 70% of the test before you take it!

Write your own questions in the textbook margins.

You gain complete control of your material by using your own organizational skills and your own instincts each step along the way.

Knowing What Is in Your Memory and What Isn't

How will writing questions in the margins make studying for tests less time consuming?

How will this affect my confidence in my memory and my knowledge?

If you're like most people, you may often think you don't know something even though you actually do. That's a shame: It's not useful to spend your time or use up self-esteem thinking you don't know something if you actually do know it. The amazingly comforting thing about writing your own questions in the margin is that when you go back to study for your test, you have already structured the material to be "study-efficient." You save time, because you only have to reread the sections in which you can't answer your own questions. Knowing that you have written the questions and that you can answer them is very reassuring. You know for sure that you really do know what you need to know. You are confident that the material is safely tucked away in your long-term memory. (To ensure that you store maximum information in your long-term memory using a minimum of time, see *Implement a Review Process for Maximal Recall in Minimal Time* in *Section 3*.)

Of course, once you experience seeing your own questions crop up in your tests, you will gain immeasurable confidence. The true joy of learning will develop within you. As you gain confidence, you'll realize that the entire world of ideas is open to you.

What is meant by "knowing that you know"?

Knowing that you know and having confidence in your own abilities will make you a first-rate learner. In so many ways, the difference between people who are successful and people who aren't is simply a matter of confidence. And confidence can be built. As a matter of fact, only you can build your own self-confidence (obviously, right?). In this and the following section, we've written the questions in the margins so you can see what it's like. Once you get the hang of it, you'll feel in control and secure in your own ability to formulate questions effectively.

What About Complex, Abstract, or Conceptual Material?

How can I make abstract concepts concrete?

Obviously, not all the material you study is concrete, purely factual. Concepts, philosophies, questions of logic, and hypotheses can all be difficult to attach a direct question to. This kind of material crops up in any field of study. In many disciplines, such as law, medicine, philosophy, literary criticism, and countless others, you encounter this kind of challenging material frequently.

You must learn in a childlike, unfearful and open way for learning to be as effective as it can be.

How do you make the abstract concrete? One very effective tip is to develop a clear picture—a visual construction—of the concept you are trying to learn. The various bits and pieces of information that make up the larger concept must be connected with one another to be understood adequately. The less form that the material you're studying has, the more its parts need to be connected.

It is very effective to construct an actual physical model to make complex or theoretical material real to you, to make it something you can literally look at, touch, turn over, move around. You physically and literally make the abstract concrete. You've seen children playing with building blocks, right? Do you remember how some of the building blocks had a letter painted on them to help kids learn spelling and construct words and phrases? Do you remember how intensely the children were involved, how completely transported and engaged they were? Well, as you think of a little kid playing, understand that you were this child! This is how *you* learned major new concepts.

How You Feel Often Determines How Well You Do

What does kinesthetic activity refer to?

What kinds of skills does kinesthetic activity help develop?

Why is "play" so important to learning?

While engaged in these physical activities, this state of pure doing, often called *kinesthetic activity* (meaning touch, physical sensations, feelings, movements, and so forth), your brain is intensely active. This kind of activity is critical to the development of your spatial and conceptual skills. In addition, the more you enjoy, relax, and totally get into the play, the better you learn, because there is no longer any barrier between doing and learning. No anxiety, no fear. This is how optimal learning takes place.

What are the advantages of "childlike" learning?

What are some barriers that "playlike" learning avoids?

Psychologists often say that play is the work of children. This doesn't just mean that playing is how children spend their time. It means that play is critically important for developing important skills and ideas. It is clear that you must learn in a childlike, unfearful, and open way for learning to be as effective and complete as it can be. Research has demonstrated this over and over again. Have you ever observed how children can learn vast amounts of information in a relatively short period of time? That's because they are engaged in pure learning. There are no barriers to learning, no insecurity, worry, fear, or boredom.

You probably gave up playing with building blocks and other

such toys because at some age, you perceived or were told that such pursuits are "childish." Of course, you wouldn't want to be viewed as "a big baby." The irony is that these forms of play are not childish. They are "childlike." And again, research demonstrates unequivocally that for everyone, including adults, learning in a childlike way is the best way to learn, to remember, and to be able to apply what you've learned to actual situations.

So get back to being childlike. Playing with toys is precisely what works when learning challenging, complex, and abstract material. Get back to it. It works as well for older kids and for adults as it does for small children. (We would all be lucky and successful if we could learn large quantities of information at the remarkable pace of young children.)

Study Tip

The next time you're unsure of how to tackle a challenging concept or a hard-to-grasp idea, literally separate it into its component parts, represented by the blocks in a LEGO or Tinker Toy set. Put the parts together with the sticks that come with the blocks. Form a physical model of connected parts that represent the concept. You can paint the blocks different colors with tempera or acrylic paint or with colored marking pens. Each color can represent the component parts of one category within the whole structure. You can also write on the blocks to indicate what each piece represents. You could mark them with colored paper or masking tape or little doodads—jewelry, paper clips, pieces of colored paper to illustrate specific details of the concept.

(You may think of this as extra "work" for you or as a game you have no time to play, but the more you play physically with information, the deeper it gets imbedded in your long-term memory.)

This is nothing new to you. Remember, you did this when you were a kid. Well, do it again. It still works. Trust your imagination, and it will serve you well. Remember though: Play at it. Have fun with it. If you aren't playing, you're not doing it right. That's the tip: Have fun with it.

What kinds of "toys" can I use to make an abstract idea concrete?

What attitudes do I bring to this kind of activity in order to make it successful for me so I can learn the challenging material?

> "*Learning is movement from moment to moment.*"
> – *J. Krishnamurti (1895–1986)*

Learning by Doing Is As Important As Learning by Seeing and Hearing

As you look at your model every day, it will gradually begin to represent the concept you are working to learn. Even if, under regular circumstances, you have a difficult time remembering this kind of information or have difficulty connecting it with other information you have already learned, this physical representation can make it real for you. Continue to move your structure around, look at it from different angles every so often. Soon, you'll be able to move it around in your mind, just as you can with graphical elements in the computer. Keep in mind that this is just another way of viewing learning. This approach is a very important, but unfortunately often ignored, learning technique (particularly with older children and adults). This is kinesthetic learning, and it is just as valid as learning that involves seeing information and hearing information. It is learning by physically doing. With abstract material and many other kinds of material, you learn much more thoroughly and with better memory than you could ever learn by thinking alone.

The more you work with each component in the LEGO set—writing information on the blocks, gluing on little pieces of colored paper or trinkets to represent some idea or component element, the more the information will be transmitted to your long-term memory. By literally doing the physical activity, you create a physical picture that you will remember when taking a test or when your job (or schoolwork) requires you to turn theory into concrete application.

Research has discovered that if you learn in a dramatic and unusual environment, the information is uplifted into your long-term memory. Clearly, building LEGO models of abstract ideas is dramatically different from most learning activities. This unusual technique really helps plant information in your long-term memory, where you can access it and depend on it.

With this technique, you turn something very abstract into something very concrete. By constructing something physical and touchable, you make it real for yourself. The expression "use it or lose it" often applies to learning. You must do something with the ideas in order to plant them firmly in your brain. Otherwise, you may lose them.

Research also demonstrates that to learn and remember with maximum effectiveness, you must experience positive emotions as you are learning. Because the music on ***Learn with the Classics*** taps into the brain's perceptions of relaxation and well-being, the music serves that purpose: It tells your brain to feel positive emotions, therefore what you learn will automatically transfer to your long-term memory. (To maximize the amount of information that stays in your memory for more complete recall, see *Implement a Review Process for Maximal Recall in Minimal Time* in *Section 3.*)

What do positive emotions have to do with memory?

What does music do that creates the positive emotions needed for good learning?

Construct a physical model to learn complex or theoretical material.

When you feel baffled by material or can't get a handle on it, make it physical, make it a "toy."

Music for Creativity

To set the stage for your creative endeavor, it's very helpful to play the right music. As you've discovered, the slow Baroque music on ***Learn with the Classics*** creates a feeling of active relaxation, ideal for this kind of activity. Two other kinds of music are also quite useful for creativity activities and for producing positive emotions. Quick Baroque music (though quicker in tempo, it still has the same qualities of structural complexity, melodic richness, and steady beat that the slower Baroque music has) can really give you a hit of focused energy. One ***Relax with the Classics*** recording, *Classical Rhythms*, is designed to give you a hit of energy without making you feel edgy or hyper. It helps "activate" the information you're working on—that is, it helps make the information a part of you—especially

To set the stage for your creative endeavor, it's very helpful to play the right music.

What are three types of music that work for enhancing creativity?

What do they do?

if you want to feel more energy. It was created to be used in all sorts of brainstorming activities, either by yourself or with others, and for kinesthetic learning. *Classical Rhythms* is also very effective to play during study breaks or in the late afternoon when energy often flags. It is ideal to play during physical exercise, because it helps you get a great workout and de-stress at the same time!

Classical Impressions, another ***Relax with the Classics*** recording, contains yet another kind of creativity-enhancing music—slow, gentle, melodic, and relaxing nineteenth- and twentieth-century classics. It is designed to evoke vivid mental pictures, with exquisite detail, depth of color, and feelings of peace and contentment. People typically picture colorful landscapes, vast meadows, gentle streams, magnificent clouds. These are all images that contribute to the positive emotions required for putting information firmly into long-term memory.

So by listening to whichever of these choices of music you feel "in tune with" at the time, you will be actively embedding information into your long-term memory as you build your LEGO model.

Somebody once asked the composer Anton Bruckner:

"Master, how, when, where did you think of the divine motif of your Ninth Symphony?"

"Well it was like this," Bruckner replied. "I walked up the Kahlenberg, and when it got hot and I got hungry, I sat down by a little brook and unpacked my Swiss cheese. And just as I open the greasy paper, that darn tune pops into my head."

– Anton Bruckner (1824–1896).

Review and Reflection

Review

Key points you've learned in Section 2:

1. Why should I write questions in the margins when I study?

- You'll make sure you've alerted yourself to each important piece of information.
- You'll make studying for tests more efficient: You'll only have to reread the sections for which you can't answer your own questions.
- You'll know what you know and what you don't know.
- You'll focus your studying on only those areas that you don't know.
- You'll build confidence in your capacity to study and in your own memory.
- You'll see, on average, 70% of your own questions on the test.

2. What does kinesthetic activity refer to?

- Touch
- Physical sensations
- Feelings
- Movements

3. What kinds of skills does kinesthetic activity help me develop?

- Spatial skills
- Conceptual skills
- Better, more complete learning

4. What are some barriers that "playlike" learning avoids?

- Insecurity
- Worry
- Fear

- Boredom

☑ 5. **What kinds of "toys" can I use to make an abstract subject concrete?**

- LEGOs
- Tinker Toys
- Tempera or acrylic paint
- Marking pens
- Doodads and trinkets
- Jewelry
- Paper clips
- Colored paper

☑ 6. **What are three types of music that work for enhancing my creativity, and what do they do?**

- Slow Baroque—creates active and alert relaxation
- Quicker Baroque—provides energy boost and activates information
- Gentle modern classics—promotes imagination and evokes vivid mental pictures

☑ 7. **What emotional condition is necessary for my long-term memory to be activated? What does music have to do with it?**

- Positive emotions are required for information to be transferred into long-term memory.
- This music automatically produces a sense of positiveness and well-being in the brain.

Reflection

In this and the following *Reflection* sections, we will suggest some topics for you to reflect on. It's also useful, however, for you just to let your mind wander sometimes, with no particular topic in mind. Remember to turn up the musical volume a bit, which will shift your brain into alpha. See where your wandering mind takes you. What images come up for you? Are some things really surprising? Interesting? Funny? If, on the other hand, your mind gets stuck playing tapes of your daily routine, if it becomes boring or frustrating, remember that the goal of reflection is to be positive and to develop new ideas and insights. So don't worry if sometimes your reflections "reflect" the mundane aspects of your life. When you do notice it though, see if you can redirect the reflection down a more positive path. If you still feel stuck, stop the reflection for a while. Approach it again later.

Now, treat yourself to a little flight of fancy. Remember a time when you learned something in a childlike, unfearful, and open way. Go back as far in time as you need to. (How far back can you remember? Sometimes, when we really let ourselves go and relax, we can remember terrific experiences that happened when we were quite little.) Reflect on how you learned back then. Remember what was so pleasurable about it. What kinds of materials, toys, or props were you using? What else contributed to the lightness and fun? Do you remember people smiling? Do you remember laughing? It's really enjoyable to recall these great learning experiences.

Now, think about the challenging subject for which you've chosen to design a study plan. Imagine yourself learning this subject in the exact same way as you did in your pleasurable memory. Picture yourself using all of the same enjoyable learning elements. Picture your current course material very specifically, and visualize how it could be learned in this fun way. When you go back to learning this subject, start applying this relaxed and open approach to your perceptions of the material. Allow the lightness and ease that you experienced in your memory to carry over into your study of this subject.

Notice any doubts or objections that your "rational" mind may raise to learning in this fun, childlike way. Consider whether these objections may be based on societal conventions, perhaps viewing this kind of fun learning as childish and silly. Consider whether part of the doubt may arise from any negativity about yourself and about things in general. Consider also whether you are motivated and committed to being a top learner.

From Learning to Doing

Let's Go

Continue building your study plan by including the study tips and learning strategies that you've discovered in this

continued next page . . .

Show Me

For those of you who need to gather more information before experimenting with the material in ***Learn with the Classics,*** keep

continued next page . . .

Let's Go . . . continued . . .

section. By including these "studying smart" techniques, you will always know what you know and know what you don't know. This will make the stressful process of cramming for tests a thing of the past and the confident, purposeful utilization of a well-prepared study plan the way of the future.

Begin writing questions in the margins of the books you use in the subject for which you have chosen to design your study plan. (Of course, if the books belong to the school, use Post-its.) Then, test your new skill by having a teacher, a friend, or a fellow student ask you questions from a section of the book where you have written the questions in the margin.

(In *Section 3,* you'll learn how to review the information for which you've written questions, so it will be in your long-term memory by the time you are ready to take a test in the subject you've chosen for your study plan.)

Show Me . . . continued . . .

reading. Start the activations suggested in the *Let's Go* sections whenever you are ready.

Remember the discussion in *Section 1* about *Show Me* people—those people who are not convinced by their own experiences but require scientific proof that something new is of value to them? Remember the discussion about people who have a hard time making decisions? Well, if you think that might apply to you, read on. It's really fun and really useful to understand ourselves, how we learn best, and what we require to make us comfortable with new ideas. We invite you to take a look at the processes that you actually use to make decisions or to convince yourself of something.

When you have a goal—becoming a great learner, for example—the steps that you take to achieve your goal are called *strategies.* We all use many different sets of strategies to get to our goals. To become a great learner, you use what is called a *learning strategy.* In using this strategy, you systematically process new information in your brain, usually by seeing or hearing the information, maybe talking to yourself about it, perhaps reading the material again, questioning the information, and so forth. You continue with this process until you feel good about the material, at which point you accept it into your memory. This is a step-by-step process, which we develop very early in life, and which we automatically—*and*

continued next page . . .

Show Me . . . continued . . .

most often subconsciously—activate every time we are presented with new information that we want to learn.

Over time, a strategy can "mutate" and separate into two branches. One of the branches works effectively, in which case learning is a snap. The other branch is ineffective, and then learning is very difficult. Such "dualistic" strategies develop unconsciously over the course of years, primarily as a result of negative experiences or a lack of self-confidence.

Strategies are a systematic way of accomplishing something by processing information and weighing it against your personal agenda; your experiences; your goals, values, morals, and beliefs; and your hopes and wishes. We use our strategies whenever we are asked questions that require answers, whenever we are presented with new ideas that require a response, and whenever we want to accomplish a goal. Often, our strategies are simply habitual, unexamined ways that we consistently do things. Frequently, the entire process takes place in seconds or even nanoseconds (which is actually a tribute to our powerful and wonderful brain!). The secret to developing effective strategies is to look at the *habitual strategies* and turn them into *purposeful strategies.*

It's fun to take a good look at the countless strategies we implement every single day. We may have a strategy for preparing a speech or for studying math, for example. We may have a strategy for cooking a great meatloaf dinner or for improving our basketball skills. Most of us have a rather detailed strategy (though generally totally habitual and unexamined) for getting out of bed in the morning. It may go something like this: You set the alarm on the clock radio the night before. You adjust the volume control and the station setting. You check the AM/PM setting. When the alarm goes off, you hit the snooze button. You nod off for 10 more minutes. The alarm goes off again. Finally, you get out of bed and go into the bathroom. Of course, *your* morning get-out-of-bed ritual is not exactly

continued next page . . .

Show Me . . . continued . . .

like this, but if you examine it carefully, you'll discover how detailed it is and probably how habitual it is.

We all have a strategy for convincing ourselves of something, called a *convincer strategy,* and one for making decisions, called a *decision strategy.* If one of the steps in your convincer strategy is always to ask yourself, "Where's the proof?" you may actually be unable to have a spontaneous experience when the absolute proof isn't available to you at that moment. This can be very limiting and can lead to skepticism of all things new. There are many wonderful new things that can bring depth and satisfaction to our lives if we can suspend the need for immediate intellectual understanding. Being overly critical and analytical keeps some people from jumping into life's challenges and opportunities. (By the way, scientific proof that music primes the brain for learning is coming up in *Section 5.*)

In most cases, the final step we take in a decision strategy or a convincer strategy is to check out our feelings: Does the decision feel right? When it feels right, we go ahead. If it doesn't feel right, we either decide against it, go ahead with it reluctantly, or (because we are unconvinced), we either postpone the decision or wind up taking no action at all. When these things happen, we can become confused and frustrated because of a lack of closure. Things feel unfinished and unsatisfying.

Oftentimes, we can't make up our minds simply because we don't have all the information needed to reach a conclusion. Notice when you feel stuck, and you can't make up your mind. Ask yourself if you have all the information you need to get to closure. If you see that you don't, just keep gathering information. It is this awareness of how you develop strategies that will allow you to take simple steps to make your strategies effective.

Some people have very effective strategies, either acquired through training they've received *(effective strategizing can be learned!)*

continued next page . . .

Show Me . . . continued . . .

or by inclination. These people can quickly and efficiently make decisions and convince themselves of something. Other people have cumbersome and ineffective strategies that slow them down and often achieve ineffective results. In either case, we should pay attention to these processes, because in many ways, they run our lives!

Begin looking at your own strategies, the habitual ones and the purposeful ones. When we become conscious of the strategies we are using, we can monitor them and modify them when they're not working the way we want them to. In this way, they become purposeful rather than habitual. This is when they become powerful and highly effective.

As you continue making up your mind about the information in ***Learn with the Classics*** and its potential benefits for you, we invite you to sit back and try one or more of the following:

1. Ask yourself what it would take for you to be convinced that studying and learning with music could be a powerful addition to your other studying techniques. Decide which of the information that you have read so far feels good to you and which doesn't. Then, you can begin to work with the information and the tools that you believe could be of value to you.

2. Think back on a time when you critiqued or analyzed some new information or unfamiliar procedures and decided to give it a try. (This could pertain to school, sports, games, personal relationships, or anything else.) Remember how good it felt to take a new approach and enrich your life. Then, remember a time when you were just plain negative and refused to try something new. Remember how that felt as well.

3. As an experiment, we invite you to suspend judgment and abandon logic and analysis just long enough to try out one of the *Let's Go* activations you've seen in ***Learn with the Classics!*** "Cherry pick"

continued next page . . .

Show Me . . . continued . . .

an activation from any of the *Let's Go* sections, one that seems interesting and worthwhile or at least not particularly troublesome for you. Then, do it! You will begin to experience a feeling of movement, of going forward—of getting unstuck—and you'll feel a sense of engagement—the exhilaration of trying something new. Go wherever it takes you and enjoy!

Resources and References

For information on *Classical Impressions, Classical Rhythms,* and other recordings in the ***RELAX WITH THE CLASSICS*** series:

LIND Institute
P.O. Box 14487, San Francisco, CA 94114
1-800-LEARN-R-US (1-800-532-7678)
From overseas: 415-864-3396
FAX: 415-864-1742, E-Mail: lind@lind-institute.com
Visit our web site at: www.lind-institute.com

See page 93 for information about these educational products.

For information and ideas on constructing LEGO models, access the LEGO web site.

The original model of Tinker Toys is available from Back to Basics Toys at www.backtobasicstoys.com, or call 1-800-356-5360.

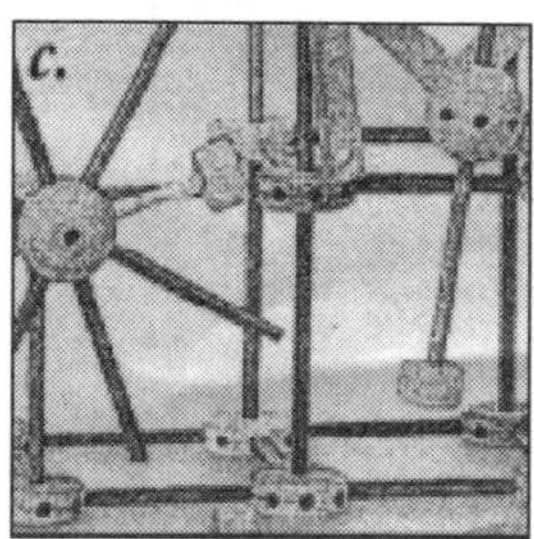

Learn to Learn Better

SECTION 3

By Knowing "Why," You'll See "How"

Preview

In this section, you will deepen your understanding of the science of the brain. As your understanding of your own brain continues to develop, your abilities to learn and remember will develop as well. You'll also discover a powerful technique that makes the most of your reviewing time.

HIGHLIGHTS

- Levels of Consciousness
- Right Brain, Left Brain, and Whole Brain
- What Your Well-Tended Brain Will Do for You
- Implement a Review Process for Maximal Recall in Minimal Time

Once you truly understand that, scientifically speaking, your brain knows all sorts of things that you don't realize it knows, you will gain confidence in your own power of learning. By employing a few simple study techniques and using the music to jump-start your brain and keep it in gear, you become aware of your brain's unbelievable capacities and discover how to tap into them.

Understanding how memory works, knowing "where" in the brain your vast storehouse of information is located, and discovering how to tap into it will continue to prove to you how great your knowledge and your memory really are. (They already are. The trick is knowing how to gain access to them.) ***Remember:*** It's also important to have confidence that you can connect what you've just learned with what you already know—what is stored in your long-term memory.

The human brain is a marvelous instrument. It has the ability to perceive and use sound vibrations to create music and to understand music, in terms of its *rhythm* (beat), *melody* (tune), *harmony* (arrangement of musical notes), and *form* (pertaining to musical structure). This capacity of your brain can have an enormous and wonderful influence on both your health and your ability to learn.

Two scientific views of the mind and the brain that reinforce the powerful effectiveness of the music are the *Levels of Consciousness* view and the *Right-Brain–Left-Brain–Whole-Brain* view.

Levels of Consciousness

We all go through three different levels of consciousness many times every single day. Most of the time, you have no control over these transitions. You will gain great power in harnessing your creativity and brainpower once you begin using music to make the transitions for yourself.

What are the three levels of consciousness?

Conscious Mind—the state of present awareness. In this state, you're completely tuned in to the current moment.

Preconscious Mind—the state that links the conscious mind and the subconscious mind. Music provides access to this in-between state of consciousness that is necessary for healthy and optimal living in general and first-rate learning in particular.

Subconscious Mind—the state that controls creative ideas, insights, and emotions. It is also where vast amounts of information are stored. Much of what you've forgotten on a conscious level is remembered in your subconscious.

What is the purpose of each of the levels of consciousness?

The preconscious mind is the least understood level of consciousness, yet it holds the key in terms of optimal learning, remembering, and creativity. When you listen to the music at an audible enough volume to really hear it well, you shift into alpha, which of course is slower and more relaxed than beta. This enables you to access the preconscious mind, through which the healthy connection between conscious and subconscious is made. So, the preconscious mind is the "door" or the "link" between the conscious and the subconscious mind. Whatever image works for you—a door, a gateway,

The preconscious mind is the "door" or the "link" between the conscious and the subconscious mind.

a train track, whatever—use it to think of the preconscious as the means to travel to and from the present (conscious mind) and the past (subconscious mind). Those of us who learn to tap into the preconscious are light-years ahead in terms of getting maximum performance from our brains.

The subconscious mind is not controlled by the conscious thinking mind. It is rich with raw insight and vision and originality as well as a vast amount of memory, which you're unaware of on a conscious level. In fact, one theory is that you never forget any sensory experience (sight, sound, touch, smell, and taste) you have ever had. To access the powerful but often hard-to-get-to subconscious, you must go through the gateway state of mind, the preconscious. Because it can tap into the preconscious, music is the key to getting to all the wonders that the subconscious mind contains. As you continue to work with music in this way and to realize how much creativity and knowledge you actually have, you will begin to trust your own ideas and thoughts, to have confidence in your own abilities as distinct from anyone else's.

What's in it for me to be able to access the subconscious?

Memory and Learning. Your subconscious holds your vast storehouse of memory. For learning, studying, taking tests, you need both to be able to remember what you've learned previously and also to connect it to what you're currently learning. Using Baroque music, you are aided in getting information in and out of your subconscious quickly, which facilitates learning the skills, ideas, and information you need to succeed in your ultimate career.

What things can the subconscious help me do?

Creativity and Originality. Highly creative people frequently shift in and out of the subconscious state. When you accomplish this shift, you gain access to the rich and unlimited originality and imagination required to make great art—paintings, poetry, stories, music of all sorts, interior design, architecture, dancing—you name it.

Expanded Possibilities for Pleasure and Fun. Through the music, which enables you to access your subconscious, you can retrieve your own highly individual wealth of knowledge, thoughts, feelings, and insights; and you can use them to develop your own personal spin on things. By bringing your unique qualities of thought and feeling to the conscious level, you can then use them, play with them, learn from them, and build on them. You can create and contribute to the world your own ideas, ideals, visions, and passions. You can take whatever it is that interests you and make the most of it.

Right Brain, Left Brain, and Whole Brain

Another way of understanding the effects that music has on your brain is to look at the Right-Brain–Left-Brain–Whole-Brain view. The same music that helps you tap into the preconscious and the subconscious and that helps you shift between beta and alpha also connects what has popularly been referred to as right- and left-brain activity. (Though this terminology is being phased out in the scientific community, we use it here for simplicity.) The kind of slow Baroque music on ***Learn with the Classics*** makes this connection extraordinarily well.

The Baroque and some classical music keep both sides of the brain working at the same time.

What is meant by right-brain, left-brain, and whole-brain learning?

Generally speaking, left-brain activity tends to involve language and logic—words, concepts, organizing information—things of that nature. Right-brain activity tends to involve pictures, feelings, and sounds—your senses, artistry, and creativity.

How can music affect the different sides of your brain?

What is it about Baroque music that sparks whole-brain learning?

When the ideal music, such as that on ***Learn with the Classics***, is used during learning and studying, both sides of your brain function simultaneously. In other words, you are using your whole brain! This cannot be said of many learning tools. Somehow, because of its complexity of form (its musical structure); its melodic richness; and its predictable, safe, and secure beat, the Baroque and some classical music (principally Mozart) keep both sides of the brain working at the same time.

Whole-brain learning is infinitely more powerful than either right- or left-brain learning. It is more complete and rounded out. You actually perceive what you're learning in greater depth. Just as you, as a person, are not one-dimensional—there are many sides to you, many moods, many talents, many ideas—so too are the concepts and information you are studying multidimensional. Just as knowing the whole you is more interesting than only knowing parts of you, so is knowing the whole of your subject more interesting than only knowing parts of it. The whole is much greater than the sum of its parts. It takes both sides of your brain to perceive the wonderful richness and wholeness of what you are studying.

When you are taught primarily in words (not pictures), as is so often the case (often in English and social studies classes, for example), if you are a word-oriented learner, you probably become alive and feel alert; you're inclined to pay attention because your left brain is being activated, and that is how you need to learn at your best. If you're a right-brain learner though, your mind is inclined to go elsewhere. You will not be engaged by words alone. On the other hand, if you are a right-brain learner, if the learning activity centers around pictures and shapes (art and geometry, for example), you feel connected and engaged. In these instances, the word-oriented, left-brain student's mind may wander. This is why it is important for teachers to teach to both styles of learners. Of course, more teachers need to get this information and understand how crucial it is.

What kinds of learning activities are in the domain of the left brain?

What learning activities typically involve the right brain?

If you are right-brain dominant, it is likely that your learning needs are often ignored, though certainly not intentionally. It's simply that a greater number of people are left-brain dominant, including a majority of teachers. That's why right-brain learning is so often ignored. Most artists, inventors, and many, if not most, scientists tend to be right-brain dominant.

When music accompanies your learning, if you are right-brain dominant, you will be able to learn because your brain is getting the stimulation it requires. The music occupies your right-brain processing, which decreases distractedness otherwise caused by right-brain activity. Your left brain can focus more on learning—reading,

What is the benefit to right-brain learners to having this music accompany their learning?

What is the benefit to left-brain students?

How is whole-brain learning superior?

memorizing, conceptualizing. If you're left-brain dominant, the music will benefit you as well, giving you a richer, more meaningful experience, because the music gets both sides of your brain involved. For both types of learners, whole-brain learning is infinitely superior, longer lasting, and more enjoyable than either right- or left-brain learning alone.

Use music to tap into both sides of the brain at the same time.

Whole brain learning is easier, more fun, and far more effective than right- or left-brain learning alone.

What Your Well-Tended Brain Will Do for You

As you've discovered, to enhance your learning, your memory, and your creativity:

- **You want your brain to shift in and out of alpha and beta.**
- **You want to use both your right and your left brain (for truly effective whole-brain learning).**
- **You want to travel freely between your conscious mind and your subconscious mind by accessing the preconscious.**
- **You want to retrieve all the information and insight contained within your brain and then to integrate it with new information and insight.**

As you become increasingly knowledgeable and practiced in using the music, your brain will respond with greater and greater efficiency and imagination.

Implement a Review Process for Maximal Recall in Minimal Time

Study Tip

Develop a systematic reviewing technique over the course of six months whenever you learn significant new information.

Each time you study new material that is important to your subject and that you want to commit to long-term memory, use this review schedule: After studying material for approximately 45 minutes, take a 10-minute break and then review the material for 5 minutes. After one day, review the material for 5 minutes. After one week, review it for 3 minutes. After one month, review it for 3 minutes. After six months, review it for 3 minutes.

According to noted Accelerated Learning expert Colin Rose, fewer than 20 minutes of review time over the course of six months time can produce a 400 to 500% increase in recall! Rose based his conclusion on the work of several other cutting-edge learning experts, including Tony Buzan and Peter Russell. It is important to follow the precise schedule to achieve maximum results. But it is an insignificant amount of time for you to spend, considering the amazing results you will get. In the long run, this approach will save you countless hours of study time, many of which are ineffective and often amount to nothing but wasted time followed by frustration. Their formula assumes an average of 45 minutes of initial study time (which is typical for most students initially studying important new material).

It's helpful to use a great big calendar hung on your wall, so you can make your schedule. As soon as you've studied your important material, take your 10-minute break, then review for 5 minutes. At that time, note on your calendar the rest of your long-term review schedule: 5 minutes the next day, 3 minutes after one week, 3 minutes after one month, and 3 minutes after six months.

What is the timetable for the powerfully effective and time-saving Accelerated Learning review process?

Follow this process faithfully after each significant study session of new and important material. You'll get a huge pay-off for your efforts.

Review important newly learned material in a systematic way over the course of six months.

It takes a total of only 20 minutes of review over the course of six months to ensure maximum information transfer from short-term to long-term memory.

Review and Reflection

Review

Key points you've learned in Section 3:

1. What are my three levels of consciousness?

- *Conscious Mind*—state of present awareness
- *Preconscious Mind*—in-between state that is the gateway to the subconscious, accessed easily with slow Baroque music
- *Subconscious Mind*—controls basic insights and emotions and houses long-term memory

2. What can I gain by accessing my subconscious?

- Vastly improved memory and first-rate learning
- Your own highly unique creativity
- Ability to connect what you've just learned with what you previously have learned
- More fun and excitement

3. What are the "parts" of my brain that are used for learning?

- Left brain
- Right brain
- Whole brain

4. What elements of Baroque music promote whole-brain learning?

- Complexity of form—musical structure
- Melodic richness
- Regular beat

5. What are some things that tend to be dominated by the left brain?

- Words

- Concepts
- Organizing information

6. What are some things that tend to be dominated by the right brain?

- Pictures
- Feelings
- Sounds

7. How does the music benefit all learners?

- It stimulates right-brain learners so they become engaged.
- It stimulates left-brain learners to benefit from the creative right-brain point of view.
- It gives everyone the benefit of using the whole brain, because the whole is greater than the sum of its parts.

8. What is the timetable for the six-month review process of significant newly learned information?

- After 10 minutes 5 minutes of review
- After 1 day 5 minutes of review
- After 1 week 3 minutes of review
- After 1 month 3 minutes of review
- After 6 months 3 minutes of review

Reflection

Remember a time when some bit of knowledge or some idea surfaced in your mind to your own great surprise. Remember how you amazed and delighted yourself that you even knew this thing or that you had remembered it at all.

From Learning to Doing

Let's Go

1. To achieve greater access to your subconscious as you use the music and during your reflections, do the following: Make a list of things that you know you must have known at one time but that you have since "forgotten": the color of your house when you were a child, the name of the first dog or cat you ever knew, the sound of your first-grade teacher's voice, your feelings at your first big Thanksgiving dinner, for example.

   Have a friend or fellow student read the list back to you as you sit comfortably and listen to the slow Baroque music. Close your eyes if you like, lie back, whatever makes you feel comfortable, relaxed, and receptive. Give yourself sufficient time to go inside yourself and look for the answers.

   It is less important that you come up with the answers than that you carefully notice the process you are engaged in. What pictures, sounds, or feelings come up? What kinds of memories does this process evoke? What information do you actually remember that you thought you had "forgotten"? If these things are still in your memory, what else might be there? (Let go of any unpleasant

continued next page . . .

Show Me

If you are ready now, experiment with the activations presented in this and the preceding chapters.

For those who require more proof, see *Section 5,* which provides evidence that some music actually makes you smarter (at least temporarily), as measured on IQ tests, and that it certainly primes your brain for learning.

Let's Go . . . continued . . .

memories or insights. Just focus on those that you like to remember and feel good about.)

With practice, such frequent "visits" to your subconscious will develop the skill of probing. Becoming more probative will result in increased and more deliberate access to information when you really need it.

2. The next time you have read a good chunk of ***Learn with the Classics,*** test out the systematic reviewing process that has been discussed in this section. Immediately after having read for 45 minutes, take a 10-minute break and then review the material for 5 minutes. After one day, review the material again for 5 minutes. Continue the process until you have completed the entire reviewing process. Then, look back and see how far you've come in your ability to remember information.

   Once you begin to get the hang of using this review schedule, apply it to the subject you've chosen for your study plan.

Resources and References

For information on Accelerated Learning review techniques:

Buzan, T. *Use Your Head.* Ariel Books, B.B.C. Publications, 1980.

Russell, P. *The Brain Book.* London: Routledge, 1980.

Rose, C., and Nicholl, M. J. *Accelerated Learning for the 21st Century.* New York: Delacorte, 1997.

The "Sound of Music": The Whys, the Hows, the Wherefores

Integrating Music into Your Learning

SECTION 4

HIGHLIGHTS

- What Is Learning-Supported Music?
- Safety and Security Lead to Freedom and Experimentation
- Music for Health and Well-Being
- The Brain Is a Kaleidoscope?

Preview

In this section, you will learn ways that you can begin to use music in your studying routine right away.

To "test-drive" what you learned in the previous section, write your own questions in the margin in this section. We've suggested some places where you can begin to get the feel of it.

Never underestimate the power of sound when it comes to brain function. Nothing is more influential than sound on the brain. Consider this: Of all the sensory input processes that go into our brains, sound processing affects more of our nervous system than any other type of input. In fact, auditory input affects 11 of the 12 nerve processes within the brain.

This is a great place for a question.

Remember: For good learning to take place, for your brain to be activated so it can retain information and develop thinking skills, you must experience positive emotions. When your brain experiences these positive emotions—which makes you feel comfortable, peaceful, and contented—an uplift of information occurs, transferring just-learned information from your conscious mind to your subconscious mind and therefore directly into your long-term memory. You retain more information and are able to use it most creatively. Your brain is operating in perfect balance—both intellectually and imaginatively. Slow Baroque music facilitates this process.

What Is Learning-Supported Music?

This is a great place for a question.

Good learning-supported music by its very nature stimulates then relaxes, stimulates then relaxes, many times shifting between alpha and beta states, continually allowing you to access your subconscious and bring data in and out, effortlessly using both sides of your brain for the ultimate whole-brain learning experience. All of this activity—traveling back and forth, shifting, moving, activating, stimulating and relaxing—gives the brain a real workout (without tiring you!). It's about the safest, most effective, and certainly the cheapest fitness program for the brain.

Baroque Music: Music That Makes You Stay Focused, Feel Good, and Do Well

The music gives messages to your brain to slow down unnecessary activity. The sounds are neither overstimulating nor understimulating, but rather are finely balanced to achieve the ideal state of alertness and calmness. When the brain "hears" these balanced sounds, it works at its best. It can easily focus, without distraction, on whatever task you tell it to focus on.

In the finest Baroque compositions, every part is melodic. (This is very reassuring to the brain.) It's easy to hum or sing along because the music is so songlike, so memorable. The brain knows what tones are coming next; there are no surprises. (This is also very reassuring to the brain.) There's also a lot going on structurally in the music, a lot of complexity. (This is very stimulating to the brain.) A lot of this activity is going on in your brain all at once, yet you feel comfortable because the melody and the secure, steady beat keep you grounded and relaxed. For the most part, there really is no other type of music that can do so much so well for your brain. (Some classical musical, in particular Mozart—discussed later—has some great benefits for learning.)

For the most part, there really is no other type of music that can do so much so well for your brain.

This is a great place for a question.

In addition, Baroque music uses essentially only one melody. It does all kinds of fascinating and fantastic things with that one melody, but it is only one melody nevertheless. The brain relaxes in the assurance that it knows what's happening with the music, which allows it to focus on the activity you want it to. Other kinds of music are wonderful, delightful, and enjoyable, but for achieving focus, Baroque music is unmatched.

Remember: One crucial activity that the brain performs well in this relaxed and alert state is carrying data to and from your long-term memory. This is why it is that when we are in a fully relaxed state, we can recall events and remember all kinds of information very easily. In a very tense state, we can't do it. Think about it: When you're engaged in activities that make you feel comfortable and relaxed, when you're enjoying yourself, your brain (if you choose to ask it to) will operate beautifully. This enables you to play games well, challenge your computer with speed and agility, increase your skill in sports. The barriers to learning come down when your brain is relaxed and humming along as it should be.

When you feel comfortable and relaxed, you can focus on whatever you're doing. This applies to leisure activities, and it also applies to learning activities—memorizing facts, creating poetry, conducting a scientific experiment, whatever. When you're not tied up in knots of tension and doubt, you become totally engaged in whatever you are doing: You focus; you have fun; you learn optimally.

This is a great place for a question.

LEARNING

STRATEGY

Use music to focus completely on your learning activity.

You "block out" any extraneous thoughts and emotions and engage totally with what you're doing.

Playing *Is* Learning

In most traditional learning settings, teaching techniques are almost exclusively left-brain, thinking activities, often called "top-of-the-head"

This is a great place for a question.

learning. This approach does not tap into the emotional part of the brain. As you know, research validates that when the area in the brain that pertains to emotions is triggered, learning becomes more significant, faster, and better retained. This is why when you're having fun (or "playing") with your computer games, your sport, or your craft, your brain is relaxed, and even though you're probably not thinking about it, your learning is first-rate.

Take this approach to all learning activities. Think of each learning experience as a game or a sport. Look at "problems" as puzzles to solve, at "obstacles" as challenges to conquer. As the music puts you into a positive emotional zone, let the kid in you come out. The kid is always in there, waiting to "play."

Make a game or a sport out of learning experiences.

Just as the challenges in games and sports are fun to surmount, so are the challenges in learning.

Safety and Security Lead to Freedom and Experimentation

As *your brain* is busy getting its good workout, being challenged, and humming along, *you* are feeling safe, secure, and completely focused! The Baroque composers had an elegant sense of style and a sense of respect for the listener. Their music shows this. These composers escort the listener into a musical passage smoothly and then escort the listener out the same way. You are supported, surrounded by a first-rate musical structure.

As the music puts you into a positive emotional zone, let the kid in you come out.

The underlying sense of security that you feel occurs primarily at the subconscious level. (Have no concern at all if you think you're not experiencing these feelings. You are. Even if you don't feel it, your brain does. It can't help it.)

Because of the music's stable, well-defined structure, you instinctively know that a musical resolution will occur. Because of the logical way the musical notes progress, Baroque music imparts to the listener a sense of security, a "knowing" that the musical passage will come to a safe, secure end. This musical release of tension transmits the message to the brain and body to release tension too.

A related concept to musical resolution concerns musical forms. The patterns and the structure of this great, time-tested musical style have come to be accepted over several hundred years as common to our experience and history. Even if we don't consciously "accept" these forms, we do "accept" them subconsciously, because they are part of our history. These musical forms are part of our "collective" musical experience as humans. Subconsciously, you rest in the confidence of recognizing these forms and patterns, knowing that they will resolve. At the same time, you can enjoy and be charmed by the music's unpredictable play with tunes.

This is a great place for a question.

We all need to sense that, by and large, we know what's going to happen and that we'll know how to handle it. Music offers us that framework, that structure. During learning, if that underlying secure *pulse* (beat) is there—the underlying sense that the music will come to a successful closure—you will feel the same way. In many instances, you come to breathe in synch with the music, having internalized its rhythmic pulse. Once you feel confident about the predictability, you're more willing to experiment, to take risks, and to satisfy another need we all have, which is for freedom. In other words: You need to feel the safety of the nest before you can fly.

This increased sense of security and self-esteem boosts your learning potential dramatically.

The Brain-Body Connection

Music also charges your motor system. The body takes its signals from the brain. Only when the brain has been activated will the body want to move. This affects body awareness, posture, and movement. The pulse of the music gives you the feeling that you're moving ahead. Often, you do actually move. Even if you can't get up from your seat, you often find yourself tapping your toe or nodding your head with the beat. Your entire body may be swaying even if you aren't aware of it.

This is a great place for a question.

It's because of this automatic reaction that most people at dances or parades can't stand still. They just can't. What's nice about the slow Baroque music is that it doesn't rush you forward, but it does offer you a sense of forward motion.

This sets off an automatic cycle: Brain charges; body moves. Body moves; brain charges. As this cycle happens, another one starts: As your brain's working out and your body's getting into the action, you start to feel pretty good, and that sense of security starts kicking in.

This is a great place for a question.

Music for Health and Well-Being

It is these qualities, among many others, that explain why this music is actually so healthful for you. Our lives these days are not terribly secure or predictable or safe, emotionally and in other ways. By bringing something into your life that gives you a sense of security, you can bridge a gap of stability that makes a wonderful difference in the development of your confidence and effectiveness. Naturally, this increased sense of security and self-esteem boosts your learning potential dramatically. Because you have this sense of well-being, you become more open to the physical effects of the music, bringing your mind and body into balance and placing you in optimal learning mode (which, fortunately for you, is optimal feeling-good mode also).

Great Music That Has Stood the Test of Time and Examination

Music is more than just another learning technique. It is part of our lives and our history. Great music connects to studying and learning by way of its meaning, its power, its quality, and its ability to affect thinking and creating. We use this music, great music—music that has stood the test of time and examination—because of its unmatched capacity to elevate us emotionally and intellectually.

Because of their perfection of form and balance, the great Baroque pieces are able to transport your brain to a world in which it can function optimally. Optimal living requires balance—among the physical, the social, the spiritual, the intellectual, and the emotional domains of our lives. The music's balanced elements can literally manipulate the cells of the brain, in a sense transporting you, temporarily, to a state of higher intellectual functioning.

This is a great place for a question.

Music Leads to Integration—to Solid Learning, to First-Rate Thinking, and to a Wealth of Creativity

As you've seen, music enables the smooth transition in and out of the conscious, the preconscious, and the subconscious states—each facilitating a different kind of learning. Good memory, good thinking, good creativity, all require an integration of these three states. It's important for all of the new bits of information that you get during any learning experience to connect with the literally billions of memory bits that you already have. The music helps you mix up the information—the old and the new—and form new combinations of knowledge, thought, and understanding.

If you are a medical student, for example, you must learn not only what a particular organ does but also how it relates to all the other anatomical parts that make up the human body. Whatever you are studying, it is crucial to put the pieces together in your mind so that you can comprehend the whole. This is true for a carpenter, an architect, a make-up artist, a sculptor, or a real estate broker. To succeed in any field, you need to integrate concepts and information. If you only see the

Often, when music is playing, the brain comes up with new ideas.

pieces of information and you never see how they're all linked up, then the information will never make complete sense to you, and you'll never be able to apply it in all the ways you want to. Music helps you make the links, so you can achieve wholeness of thought, understanding, and practical application.

The Brain Is a Kaleidoscope?

Think of your brain as a kaleidoscope. Kaleidoscopes work with a certain amount of raw components—chips and snippets of plastic or crystal, for example. When you add a new chip, the kaleidoscope can make all sorts of new combinations. For these new combinations to occur, however, you need to turn and twist the instrument, to manipulate it and work with it. Then you're able to get all these new perspectives and new combinations.

That's what music does to your brain. It periodically takes the brain into the preconscious state—the mixing state or moving state of consciousness—where the new chip mixes with the chips that are already there. Often, when music is playing, the brain comes up with new ideas. The music gives you that little turning of the kaleidoscope. Just as with a fine kaleidoscope, the brain that is honed and fed in this way is capable of creating endless possibilities so extraordinary that we cannot even imagine what each of us is capable of doing. But we must give our brains the fuel they need, just as the kaleidoscope maker must use the finest and most sensitive materials.

This is a great place for a question.

Step by Step: When to Play the Music for Optimal Studying and Learning

As a Prelude (introduction). *Play it before you study.* This will focus you on what you're getting ready to learn. The music gets your brain and your body primed by inducing the most receptive brain wave state. The brain requires an electrical charge to activate it. One of the most efficient ways to do this is with sound. So before you even start, the music meets this important need: It gets your brain charged. The music sets the tone for good, sound learning. Generally speaking, turn up the volume somewhat as you're preparing to study. Closing

This is a great place for a question.

your eyes, reclining in a comfortable place, just drifting with the music are all helpful and effective.

As a Support (foundation). *Play it while you study.* Once the tone is set, the music keeps your brain and body in gear, cruising along in prime learning mode. It holds and supports you in the most effective learning state. By providing the comforting support, it helps you absorb and remember what you're experiencing. It is also a psychological support, a solid foundation of sound on which good learning can be built. The music can also be the background that masks out other sounds that might distract you. Because of its wide, rich spectrum of sounds and its balance of low and high frequencies, the music activates your brain's neural impulses in a wide spectrum, which continues to keep the brain charged electrically. Generally speaking, while you're studying, keep the volume low but audible. Turn it up if there are distracting noises competing for your attention.

This is a great place for a question.

As a Finale (closing). *Play it as you finish studying.* You need a learning experience to be rounded out, completed, to give you the feeling of successful accomplishment. In many environments, the learning experience stops abruptly. (Think of the school bell or the kitchen timer going off. It's harsh, abrasive, startling.) Your brain dislikes this and won't perform optimally under such conditions. When the learning experience fades out gradually though (as when the music comes to a gradual close), you get a chance to make closure in your own being. The brain responds beautifully to this. You then have the time and the condition to integrate what you've just learned in your short-term learning experience with what you already know and then to transfer the new material into your long-term memory. This is using your brain optimally. Music gives you the chance to make that transition to integration.

This is a great place for a question.

You need this kind of closure if you are ending your study of one subject and going to another or if you are completing your studies for the day. When you are approaching closure, turn the music down in volume gradually and then turn it off, ending with a moment of quiet reflection.

Use music step by step as you study—as a prelude, a foundation, and a finale

Used systematically, music supports you in each phase of learning: to focus you, to keep you in optimal study mode, and to integrate what you've learned with what you already know.

Study Tip

As you study, it's important to take regular breaks. This gives the brain a breather. The brain enjoys short breaks every 15 minutes and a longer break every 45 minutes. By taking frequent breaks, you allow the brain to relax. This increases its performance. You will also benefit from getting more oxygen to your brain during your breaks. Oxygen is carried through your blood to your brain, so your brain would love it if you got out of your chair and stretched a bit. It's useful to step outside, take some deep breaths of fresh air. This will quickly rush a fresh supply of oxygen to your brain.

This is a great place for a question.

Remember: When taking study breaks, you might try turning the music up a little louder. Reflect a bit on what you've been studying, and focus on your breathing. It might inspire you during some breaks to listen to some different music, some of your favorites that always make you feel good and uplifted and will take your mind off your studying for a little while.

These recommendations about when to play the music, about its volume, and about the intervals for taking breaks are not written in stone. They're suggestions (though based on considerable research about what works for most people). You are an individual, who can tailor this musical tool to suit your own style. Experiment with playing the music before, during, and as you end your studying sessions, as well as on breaks and reflections. Play with the volume settings. Try listening before you study. Perhaps turn the music off while you study (or turn it way, way down). Then maybe turn it back on as you're finishing your activity. Possibly, turn it up considerably as you reflect for a few minutes. Play with it. It's up to you. You'll soon find your own rhythm.

> ***"A single human brain has a greater number of possible connections among its nerve cells than the total number of atomic particles in the universe."***
>
> *– National Academy of Sciences*

Review and Reflection

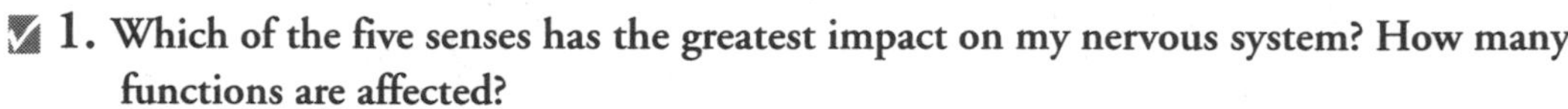

Review

Key points you've learned in Section 4:

1. Which of the five senses has the greatest impact on my nervous system? How many functions are affected?

- Sound has the greatest impact on the nervous system.
- Sound affects 11 out of a total of 12 nerve processes.

2. What must good learning-supported music do?

- It must continually stimulate and relax.
- It must shift many times between alpha and beta.
- It must involve both right and left brain.

3. What exactly is it about the best Baroque compositions that make them ideal for learning?

- Every part is melodic (reassuring to the brain).
- There is a lot going on structurally (stimulating to the brain).
- There is a secure and continuous beat (keeping you grounded and relaxed).

4. What kinds of activities will I improve in if I'm in a fully relaxed state?

- Remembering facts
- Recalling events
- Playing computer and non-computer games
- Playing sports
- Learning information and ideas

5. What is it that's so "great" about the so-called great music, taking it beyond being just another learning technique?

- It is a rich and abiding part of our history and our collective lives.

- It has great and profound meaning.
- It has a complex and challenging structure.
- It is of such undeniably high quality that it has lasted for hundreds of years.
- It elevates us emotionally and intellectually.

☑ **6. What automatic body responses does the music generate?**

- Toe tapping
- Head nodding
- Body swaying
- Can't sit still

☑ **7. What are the automatic cycles that the music triggers?**

- Your brain charges: your body moves.
- Your body moves: your brain charges.
- You feel good: you feel secure.
- You feel secure: you learn better.

☑ **8. What aspects of life must be balanced to live life at its peak?**

- Physical domain
- Spiritual domain
- Social domain
- Emotional domain
- Intellectual domain

☑ **9. How does the balance in Baroque music affect my brain?**

- The carefully balanced elements manipulate your brain cells.
- It transports you temporarily to a higher state of intellectual functioning.

☑ **10. How is my brain like a kaleidoscope?**

- Both have many raw elements.

- Both combine their elements to form new combinations.
- Both benefit by integrating new bits, which contribute to many more possible combinations.
- Both need to be manipulated, turned, twisted, handled correctly to make new combinations.
- Both need to be honed and fed to reach the potential of their creative capacity.

☑ 11. **What functions can the music serve in terms of when I play it for studying?**

- As a prelude (introduction)
- As a support (foundation)
- As a finale (closing)

☑ 12. **How does the music function as a prelude to my studying?**

- It charges your brain.
- It sets the tone for good learning.
- It provides focus.

☑ 13. **How does the music function as a support for my studying?**

- It heightens your memory.
- It provides a sense of safety and security.
- It masks distracting noises.
- It keeps your brain charged electrically.

☑ 14. **How does the music function as a finale to my studying?**

- It brings closure to your learning activity.
- It exits the activity in a calm, pleasant way.
- It allows you time to integrate just-learned information with previously learned information in your long-term memory.
- It creates the time and space for you to reflect and integrate.

☑ **15. How often should I take breaks?**

- Short breaks after 15 minutes
- Longer break after 45 minutes

Reflection

To identify the kind of positive emotions you need to have for optimal learning, sit back, play the music, and remember a time when you learned something really well or a time when you were rewarded with a kind word or an approving nod or smile. Remember how that experience gave you a great feeling. You can feel it again right now because the experience has actually stayed with you all this time. Practice reaching this feeling often by using the music and reflecting, so you can have it available at will.

From Learning to Doing

Let's Go

1. Whenever your mood seems to go down and your positive emotions seem to decrease, here's a short and effective exercise that will quickly restore positive emotions and elevate your mood, which of course are the conditions necessary for optimal learning to take place. The technique is called *clear the deck:*

   If you have had a stressful and negative experience just prior to learning or while you are learning, say to yourself, "Clear the deck!" As you say it, allow yourself to empty your mind of negative thoughts and self-defeating internal dialogue. Allow yourself to gradually let go of your negative mood, which results from stress, from pessimistic internal

continued next page . . .

Show Me

See *Section 5.* Proof is on the way.

Let's Go . . . continued . . .

dialogue, or from hearing negative comments from others.

The way to do this is to tell yourself that there is nothing you can do about the cause of the stressful situation right at that moment, while you are engaged in learning. Right? You really can't, not right then. So you may as well choose to be positive *during* the learning session and deal with the situation *after* the learning session.

Begin to develop an image in your mind that you can call upon, an image that always will make you feel good—maybe a pastoral country scene, green fields and crisply clean air, or perhaps a sandy white beach with sparkling, crystal-clear blue water. Get used to calling upon this calming and positive image whenever you need to lift your spirits as you "clear the deck." You may even want to orchestrate your image by associating it with music that you often sing or hum when you're feeling good or want to feel better. The more detailed and delightful the image, the more you let your imagination work for you, and the more you'll be able to clear the deck and create a good learning environment for yourself—even following a negative experience. Clearing the deck can free you of worry and help you stay positive, focused, and ready to learn.

You might be wondering: "How can I empty my mind of its insistent internal chatter, so that I *can* clear the deck?" Try this: Repeat the number "one" over and over again, softly, in you mind. You'll find that you cannot repeat that word continuously and think at the same time.

This technique will also work well for you at times when you don't want to listen to negative conversation from others or to information that you don't need and that will just clutter up your mind. Be selective in what you listen to.

In this Information Age, there is and will continue to be more information available than any one person needs to know at any one time. We must know how and where *to find* all of this information, not to memorize every factoid that comes our way. It is in the process of discerning what information *we really need to know* and what information *we only need to find when necessary* that makes for a discriminating learner. Look at it this way: Just as there is often the need to know, there is often *the need not to know.* Be selective in what you memorize.

continued next page . . .

Let's Go . . . continued . . .

2. Start using music regularly as a prelude (introduction), as a support (foundation), and as a finale (closing) in studying the subject for which you have chosen to design your study plan.

Resources and References

Black, S. The Musical Mind. *The American School Board Journal,* Jan. 1997, 20–22.

Harvey, A. "On Understanding the Brain's Response to Music." *International Brain Dominance Review,* 1985, *2* (1), 32–39.

Harvey, A. "Music and Health." *International Brain Dominance Review,* 1987, *4* (2), 9–12.

Rose, C., and Nicholl, M. J. *Accelerated Learning for the 21st Century.* New York: Delacorte, 1997.

Wolfgang Amadeus Mozart

1756-1791

The Mozart Effect

The Ultimate in Music That Makes You Smarter

SECTION 5

HIGHLIGHTS

- So What Can the Mozart Effect Do for You?
- Reading Challenging Material
- The Mozart Studies
- Connection Between Music, Math, and Chess

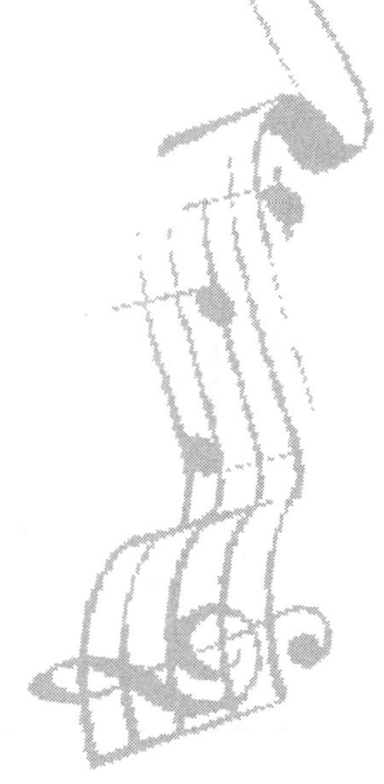

Preview

In this section, you will learn about the unique powers of Mozart's music. You'll learn how to use it and how to create a fitness program for your brain.

Practice writing your own questions in the margin in this section. (There are no prompts, as in Section 4. So, it's entirely up to your judgment.) You've already test-driven this technique, so now it's time to take it on the open road and see how it handles.

What Exactly Is the Mozart Effect?

It's been all over the news for the past several years. You may have read about it in the papers or heard about it on TV. It's called the *Mozart Effect.* What is it? Well, it refers to a phenomenon measured in two scientific studies in which *listening to Mozart actually made people measurably smarter!* These studies were conducted at the University of California, Center for the Neurobiology of Learning and Memory in Irvine. In both the first test and the second—a much larger and more controlled test—after 10 minutes of listening to Mozart, college students' IQs rose on spatial IQ tests by nine points! *It is this significant bump in IQ that is called the Mozart Effect.*

The effect was only temporary, but speculation has soared that listening to Mozart for longer than ten minutes may have a longer-lasting effect on IQ. Even more important, the implications for all of us who want to improve learning—teachers, businesses, students, and parents—are vast. Fortunately, these studies have sparked further research into the amazing connections between music and learning.

So What Can the Mozart Effect Do for You?

The nature of the studies is described later in this section, but for now, pay attention to what the researchers say about why this music works. Gordon Shaw, a theoretical physicist and one of the designers of the studies, thinks that Mozart's music may "warm up the brain." As he puts it, "We suspect that complex music facilitates certain complex neuronal patterns involved in high brain activities like math and chess. By contrast, simple and repetitive music could have the opposite effect."

Mozart's music primes the brain to perform the kind of brain activity required for complex mathematical thinking.

To warm up *your* brain, put on the ***Learn with the Classics*** recording right now. Go to **cut number 12**, and turn down the volume so that it is audible but not intrusive. That way, as you read about the Mozart Effect, you can experience the Mozart Effect.

In non-science-speak, what Shaw is saying is that Mozart's music *exercises* the brain. Because of its particular structure, it primes the brain to get into a groove in which it is capable of much higher functioning. There is a definite link between the kind of activity that Mozart's music primes the brain to perform and the kind of brain activity required for complex mathematical (and by extension, scientific) thinking. Scientists call it *spatial ability* or *spatial intelligence.* This has to do with the ability to perceive shapes and patterns, to discern how they occupy space, and to organize and move the shapes around. Some of the obvious fields of study that require this kind of thinking are geometry, physics, calculus, architecture, chess, computer science, engineering, and chemistry. These are just the obvious ones. As you probably know, spatial intelligence is key to all the best jobs in the technological marketplace. This requirement will only increase as time goes by.

College Students, Graduate Students, and Others Exposed to the Lecture Method of Teaching: Take Note, Take Caution, and Take Action

If you're in college or graduate school, you are most likely taught primarily by the lecture method. If you go to business symposiums and trainings, you too are likely to get a lot of lectures. Some of you in high school may be experiencing this already. Some of the common "symptoms" experienced by students who attend lectures are:

- Sleepiness
- Irritation
- Anxiety
- Haziness
- Wandering mind
- Checking the time repeatedly
- Inability to remember much information that the lecturer talked about
- Dual attention: trying to listen and take extensive notes at the same time

The more complex and sophisticated the material being taught, the more likely it is that it will be taught in the one of the least effective ways—the lecture. For most people most of the time, lectures can be boring, easy to tune out, hard to concentrate on, and difficult to recall. They do nothing to promote whole-brain learning and nothing to place information in long-term memory.

The most effective way to learn from lectures is by taking notes through *mind mapping*. Mind mapping is a technique that uses words, images, colors, and symbols to organize information around a central image. It's fast; it's fun; and it's an extension of the learner's way of understanding information (See *Resources and References* on page 79 to obtain more information about mind mapping.)

Remember: The "fun and games" approach to learning is the key to optimal retention, understanding, and the ability to apply what you have learned to actual situations.

Turn Left-Brain Learning into Whole-Brain Learning

You can't do much about the fact that the material you need to learn is being taught in an ineffective way. You can compensate though. Because we know that Mozart's music has been proven to increase IQ temporarily and because we know that it triggers right-brain learning, it is really useful to listen to Mozart before you go to classes that are taught primarily to the left-brain (such as lectures) or to classes in which the subject matter requires whole-brain thinking (such as mathematics and sciences).

As discussed in *Section 3,* it is really beneficial to engage the right side of the brain when you're involved in left-brain learning activities (like listening to lectures, identifying grammatical structures, organizing and writing essays and term papers, plotting outlines, memorizing facts). The music occupies your right brain, so it doesn't distract your left brain from processing facts. This gives you the powerful *whole-brain learning experience.*

Study Tip

To prime your brain's spatial intelligence, listen to Mozart before going to math and science classes and to lecture classes. On the ***Learn with the Classics*** recording, the Mozart pieces are **cuts 12 to 15**. Play Mozart in the background when preparing for a lecture class or when reading complex or deadly dull material.

Reading Challenging Material

When you're reading academic material or even recreational material that is challenging and yet not that absorbing, play Mozart softly in the background. You know the kind of reading material that you want to read or need to read but yet your mind keeps wandering when you do read it? Because of its ability to focus you, Mozart played softly in the background will gently occupy your wandering right brain and allow your left brain to concentrate on the demanding material you're reading. Not only will your concentration improve, but your memory of what you read will be better too.

In particular, the areas in which it is especially effective to listen to Mozart are:

- **Spatial learning** (such as geometry, algebra, and physics)—Listen to Mozart while doing these activities and before going to classes that teach them.
- **Before taking tests**—Listen for ten minutes or more just before enetering the test location. (This will help you infinitely more than last-minute cramming, which for most people is counterproductive.)
- **Before lecture classes**—Listen for at least ten minutes.
- **Learning and playing chess**—Play softly in the background.
- **Increasing focus and concentration**—Play softly in the background.
- **Boosting productivity and performance**—Play softly in the background.
- **Reading complex or demanding material**—Play softly in the background.

LEARNING

STRATEGY

Use Mozart to boost IQ before taking tests, to prepare for classes that require spatial intelligence, to engage the right brain before attending left-brain–oriented classes, and while reading left-brain–oriented material.

continued next page . . .

Learning Strategy . . . continued . . .

Although the slow Baroque music is wonderful for most studying and learning activities, by adding Mozart to your toolbox of musical learning utensils, you'll get the extra added brain stimulus that Mozart's music in particular offers.

Understand that the implications of the Mozart studies are well beyond improving performance on spatial tasks. The studies strongly imply that this music helps the brain perform abstract reasoning better. Period. Abstract reasoning—the ability to conceptualize, to draw inferences, to theorize, to make logical leaps in your thinking—is key to all high-level disciplines. For example:

- Comprehending and evaluating the wisdom of universal literary metaphor—absorbing the insights of great writers, such as Shakespeare, Tolstoy, and Hawthorne and applying the lessons of great literature to enriching your own life
- Deciphering and utilizing economic, scientific, and philosophical theory—understanding and applying the principles of society's greatest and most influential thinkers, such as Descartes, Voltaire, and Einstein, and determining how to shape and develop your own philosophy and worldview to function most effectively in the complex global community
- Grasping sophisticated technological principles and concepts—preparing yourself to learn about software development, engineering concepts, internal computer languages, such as Windows and Java, and building career opportunities for yourself in the technology-driven future

The Mozart Studies

In two studies, one in 1993 and one in 1994, researchers at UC Irvine set about to determine if listening to Mozart could improve university students' scores on a spatial intelligence IQ test. The test they used is part of the Stanford-Binet Intelligence Scale, a very commonly used intelligence test that many of you have probably taken.

Connection Between Music, Math, and Chess

The researchers tell us, "There are many correlational, historical and anecdotal accounts of relationships and similarities between mathematics, music and chess. A high percentage of gifted individuals are skilled in more than one of these areas, and some research studies in child development have shown correlations between music training (and musical aptitude) and measures of spatial reasoning ability. The ancient Greek Pythagoreans considered music one of the four branches of mathematics."

The purpose of their studies was "to test the hypothesis that music and spatial task performance are *causally* related [one causes the other]." They proposed that musical activity and other higher brain functions share the same nervous system firing patterns and use the same regions of the brain to perform. They predicted that "the music/spatial causal relationship is due to the cultivation of pattern development by groups of neurons brought about by musical operations."

Learning, Rhythm, and Shakespeare?

The Shakespeare Effect

To support the notion that Mozart's music is truly special in what it can do for us, it's interesting to make a comparison with another master of the arts, William Shakespeare. In the book *The Mozart Effect,* Don Campbell talks about a view held by some scholars that the precise rhythm in which Shakespeare usually wrote (iambic pentameter), when read aloud, mirrors the human heartbeat, thereby having a beneficial effect on mind and body. Campbell says that music historians often call Mozart the "Shakespeare of opera."

The Rhythm Effect

Campbell also discusses how to use rhythm as a tool to develop memory. He says it is possible to learn more information when it is learned in a rhythm or pattern. Why don't you try it some time? When you have to memorize a lot of facts or maybe equations or spelling words or special terms, put on some music that you find has a very strong beat (but not so distracting that you actually "have to listen to it"). As you set about to memorize the material, let yourself feel the beat of the music, and either think the terms in the same rhythm as the music or actually say the information out loud in time to the music.

What they are saying is that *the music actually causes the brain cells to organize in these desirable, highly effective patterns.*

The first study took place on one day. The second study took place over a period of several days. In the second study, the researchers compared the results of three different groups: one group listened to Mozart; one group listened to a combination of sounds (a different sound each day), including new age music, dance music, and stories; one group experienced silence.

Only the students who listened to Mozart experienced the significant bump in IQ. Those who listened to other sounds or to silence did not. In both studies: *Those who listened to a Mozart sonata for 10 minutes experienced a short-term increase of 9 points on the spatial IQ reasoning test.*

According to researcher Frances H. Rauscher, "Everybody is intrigued by this study because it fits everyone's intuition about music and mathematics."

The researchers believe that music can access important and complex brain patterns, can enhance the brain's ability to perceive and work with patterns, and that it can improve higher brain functioning. They believe that music can organize the brain, keeping it in tune so that it can operate efficiently and with maximum productivity. That's where we get the idea that Mozart actually makes you smarter.

The incredible connections and interlinkages between music and the brain appear to be key to unlocking some of the powerful secrets of our magnificent brain.

Mozart's Music and the Brain: What's the Connection?

What's the connection? The answer is in the question. The connection is (quite literally) the brain connections. It seems that Mozart's music literally causes the brain to go into action, connecting different cells and creating connective pathways between different parts of the brain. Apparently, the particular way that much of Mozart's music is organized is in the exact same pattern that the brain's pathways must be organized in order to perform high-level spatial and abstract reasoning functions.

Components of Music Probably Correspond to Spatial Understanding of Pattern Perception

Researchers Wendy Boettcher, Sabrina S. Hahn, and Gordon L. Shaw look at it this way: "Music, simply defined, is an ordered pattern of sounds. While music itself is very complex, it can be analyzed in terms of three primary musical structures—melody, harmony, and rhythm. Each of these structures possesses its own types of patterns."

Why Mozart?

Scientists suspect that the particular combination of rhythms, melodies, harmonies, and high frequencies that Mozart (and Mozart alone) used can uniquely stimulate the creative right-brain areas of the brain. Research into sound processing itself reveals that sounds in the high-frequency range are vastly more stimulating to the brain than lower frequencies. They are also more focusing to the brain. Mozart's music is jam-packed with high-quality high frequencies. The music does for the brain what a fantastic breakfast and an invigorating workout do for the body. Food and exercise are body fuel. Mozart is brain fuel.

The "Rosetta Stone"

The incredible connections and interlinkages between music and the brain appear to be

Another Mozart Study

While not as well-known and not as sophisticated, another Mozart study was conducted by David Merrill, a senior at Nansemond River High School in Virginia, who sought to find out if there was a difference in the effect on mice of different kinds of music. He began by running 72 mice through a maze. On average, they took 10 minutes to complete the maze. Next, he divided the mice into three groups. One group listened to heavy metal music; one group listened to Mozart; one group didn't listen to any music. After four weeks, he ran the mice through the maze again. *The heavy-metal listeners took 30 minutes to run the maze;* the silence group took 5 minutes; *the Mozart group took 1½ minutes!*

Remember: Most scientists believe that the complexity of the music is key to aiding intelligence and performance. Mozart's music (and Baroque) provide the necessary structural complexity.

key to unlocking some of the powerful secrets of our magnificent brain. The Mozart-and-spatial-intelligence research team think that the brain's response to music is the "Rosetta Stone" for the "code" or internal language of higher brain function.

Are you familiar with the Rosetta Stone? It's an ancient black slab of stone (from about 195 B.C. and discovered in 1799 in Rosetta, Egypt) with characters on it in several early "languages." When it was finally deciphered, it unlocked the code of Egyptian written language—the until-that-time indecipherable "hieroglyphics," previously seen as impossible-to-understand squiggles. Well, Mozart's music could be to unlocking the mysteries of the brain what the Rosetta Stone was to solving the mysteries of the ancient language that revealed to the world the profound body of knowledge of ancient Egypt.

The UC Irvine researchers took a major step in making the musical-brain connection—which may be the first step in breaking the code—when they determined that the brain *literally* "makes its own music." The team used a computer-generated model of neural firing patterns (electrical brain activity). They fed various brain patterns through a synthesizer. They then heard recognizable sounds of different kinds of music. Some sounded like Baroque, some like folk music, some like Eastern music. This implies that in a certain important way *brain activity is music!*

Play Mozart to exercise and develop your brain. Once in a while, play this music for no other reason than to feed your brain.

For the sheer joy and benefit of feeding your brain, simply listen to Mozart on a regular basis. Let your brain do the work while *you* relax, hang out, fool around on the computer, or whatever you do for relaxation and recreation.

Schools That Are Taking Action Now

A number of schools have introduced Mozart music as background, and they report increased attention and performance among their students.

Two educators who take the Mozart Effect seriously:

- Principal of Charleston, South Carolina, Ashley River Elementary School, Jayne Ellicott: "When our students come to school in the morning, they have to meet in the cafeteria, read a book and listen to classical music."

- Dr. Sarah Jerome, superintendent of the Kettle Moraine School District in Wisconsin: "We have given a CD of Mozart's *Sonata in D Major for Two Pianos* to almost every teacher in the district. We want to spread the Mozart word."

It's still not known the amount to which listening to Mozart can actually permanently build your brain, develop your brain, or "grow" your brain once you're no longer a child. It's clear though that it can help, maybe a lot. It definitely exercises your brain in ways that are most beneficial to its performance.

Mozart and Math

According to one biography of Mozart: Until he was about six, Mozart was totally involved in music. He then discovered mathematics and became totally absorbed in it. He scribbled figures all over the house—on walls, floors, tables, chairs. Later, he went back to music as his primary interest in life, but he always retained an interest in mathematics. Music scholars believe his remarkable musical powers were influenced by his passion for and understanding of mathematics.

Several researchers (Boettcher, Hahn, and Shaw) would like to see "super-friendly" computer games developed that could enhance conceptual and reasoning skills. In their view, these games should incorporate both music and spatial activities. They believe that this type of tool could promote the development of many forms of higher brain functioning.

Parents-of-Small-Children Alert

It is known that playing Mozart for infants and toddlers will literally develop their brains. (There's growing evidence that it works for babies in utero too.) Play Mozart often for your little ones, especially while they're playing. Play slow Baroque for them when they're cranky. It often calms them down.

One elected official, Georgia's Governor Zell Miller, is so convinced of the power of great music to influence intelligence that he used $105,000 of state money to give a tape of classical music to the parents of all newborns upon the babies' release from the hospital. Governor Miller told Georgia lawmakers, "No one doubts that listening to music, especially at a very early age, affects the reasoning that underlies math and engineering and chess." He said, "I believe it can help Georgia children to excel."

One of the ***Relax with the Classics*** recordings, *Classical Harmonies,* is all Mozart. It has been designed specifically to be used for learning and studying as described in this section.

Commit to a Fitness Program for Your Brain

According to Dr. Mark Tramko, a neuroscientist at Harvard Medical School, "There's an overlap in the brain mechanism—in the neurons used to process music, language, mathematics and abstract reasoning." According to Dr. Tramko, "We believe a handful of neural codes is used by the brain, so exercising the brain through music strengthens other cognitive skills. It's a lot like saying, 'If you exercise your body by running, you enhance your ability not only to run but also to play soccer or basketball.'"

The implications are clear: Listening to music that exercises the brain improves brain "fitness." This means the brain will perform better at other intellectual activities because it's "in good shape," so to speak. We know that Baroque music gives the brain a great workout. We also know, from Rauscher and Shaw's studies, that Mozart's music provides a great workout, probably in its own unique ways. Mozart's music possesses a unique combination of elements, including complexity of form, richness of high frequencies, and a never-to-be-heard-before-or-since play of tunes that express great wit and charm, and a deceptive simplicity.

LIND's Effective and Easy 4-Part Fitness Program for the Brain

1. **Slow Baroque** for studying, reflecting, activating newly learned information, and relaxing

2. **Mozart** for brainstorming, reading, listening to before tests and before math and science classes and lectures, and for pure brain exercising

3. **Quick Baroque** for brainstorming, energy boosts, kinesthetic learning, and physical exercise

4. **Nineteenth- and twentieth-century romantic and impressionistic** pieces for relaxing, inducing imagination and creativity, evoking imagery, creative writing, and for quiet reflection

Include each of these four types of music in your intellectual activities and in your personal activities too. You may start with the slow Baroque and the Mozart that come with ***Learn with the Classics.*** Do this with consistency and regularity. As time goes on, you'll be able to fine-tune your "exercise program" to suit your individual preferences and to correspond with what gives you the best results.

Review and Reflection

Review

Key points you've learned in Section 5:

1. What is the Mozart Effect? How did it come to be known?

- The Mozart Effect means that listening to Mozart makes you smarter.
- The effect was measured by researchers at the University of California, Irvine.

2. What exactly did the studies consist of? What exactly did they show?

- College students took spatial intelligence tests after listening to Mozart music for 10 minutes.
- In one of the studies, another group of students listened to other kinds of sounds, and still another group listened to silence.
- The IQs of the students who listened to Mozart went up 9 points on a spatial intelligence test.
- The IQs of the other students did not go up.

3. How do scientists think the Mozart Effect works?

- Mozart's music shares the same brain patterns as some types of complex brain activities.
- To perform higher-level brain functioning, the brain has to perform in the same way it does to listen to Mozart's music.
- Because of its complexity, the Mozart music "exercises" the brain.
- The exercise "warms up" the brain to perform other activities.

4. What is "spatial intelligence" and "spatial activity"?

- The ability to perceive shapes and patterns
- The ability to see how shapes and patterns occupy space
- The ability to move shapes and patterns around

☑ **5. What are some of the disciplines that require spatial intelligence?**

- Mathematics (geometry and trigonometry, for example)
- Chess
- Science (physics and chemistry, for example)
- Architecture
- Engineering
- Computer Programming

☑ **6. What are some of the "symptoms" of attending left-brain–oriented classes (such as some lectures)?**

- Sleepiness
- Irritation
- Anxiety
- Haziness
- Wandering mind
- Checking the time repeatedly
- Inability to remember much information that the lecturer talked about
- Dual attention: trying to listen and take extensive notes at the same time

☑ **7. How can listening to Mozart before math and science classes and before lecture classes help me?**

- Temporarily raises your IQ
- Occupies your right brain, which prevents left-brain distraction
- Promotes optimal whole-brain learning

☑ **8. In what learning areas is it beneficial for me to listen to Mozart?**

- Spatial learning activities
- Before taking tests
- Before lecture classes

- Learning and playing chess
- Increasing focus and concentration
- Boosting productivity and performance
- Reading complex or demanding material

☑ **9. What are some other learning activities that require abstract reasoning?**

- Understanding literature and interpreting its metaphors and universal messages
- Comprehending economic, scientific, and philosophical theory
- Grasping technological principles and concepts

☑ **10. What does Mozart's music actually do to my brain?**

- Organizes the brain's firing patterns
- Produces the conditions necessary for higher-level brain functioning
- Causes new brain connections to be made and new pathways to be formed
- Improves the brain's ability to focus
- Improves the brain's capacity to draw insights

☑ **11. What is the "Rosetta Stone," and how does it apply to Mozart and the brain?**

- It is an ancient slab of stone that, when decoded, revealed the meaning of Egyptian hieroglyphics.
- It led to the discovery of the profound body of knowledge produced by the ancient Egyptians.
- Brain activity is actually identical to music, and Mozart's music may be the key (or the "Rosetta Stone") to unlocking its secret language.

☑ **12. What complex elements in Mozart's music combine to make it such unique brain fuel?**

- Rhythms
- Melodies
- Harmonies

- High frequencies

13. How can Mozart be used to develop the brain?

- Play it frequently and regularly as a scheduled "exercise program" for the brain.
- Play it often to babies and toddlers to develop their brains (literally).
- Play it to babies in utero to begin the earliest-possible brain development.

14. What kind of music does the four-part fitness program comprise? For what activities should I use each type of music?

- Slow Baroque—studying, reflecting, activating new information, relaxing
- Mozart—brainstorming, reading, before tests, before math and science classes and lectures, pure brain exercising
- Quick Baroque—brainstorming, energy boosts, kinesthetic learning, physical exercise
- Nineteenth- and twentieth-century classics—relaxing, inducing imagination and creativity, evoking imagery, creative writing, quiet reflection

Reflection

Turn on the recording. Go to any point you choose between cut 12 and cut 15. Simply listen to the music and allow it to do its work for you. Observe your thinking process and your physical sensations. Reflect on Mozart's music and its unique and wonderful capacity to "warm up your brain." Reflect on the fact that, even now as you listen, your brain is working hard and yet effortlessly to be at its most productive and creative.

Reflect on what you now know about Baroque music and about Mozart's music. What are the differences in the way you feel or the way your thinking operates when you listen to these two kinds of music? How exactly do you experience Mozart's music differently from the way you experience Baroque music? Imagine using each type of music in your own studying. How might you use each for your own learning purposes?

From Learning to Doing

Let's Go

1. Listen to the Mozart section of ***Learn with the Classics, The Recording*** for 10 minutes before your next study session.

   Observe your feelings during and after your study session. Did you feel more in tune with the material, with the process of studying? Did you perhaps have less difficulty understanding some of the information? Did you feel more connected to it than you ordinarily would? Repeat this exercise several times during the next few weeks, and continue to pay attention to your own responses.

2. Listen to the Mozart section of the recording before one of your next tests so that you can feel calmer and more confident and so your brain can get "warmed up." You can do this in any or all of the following ways that are possible, based on the amount of time you have before and between classes:

   a. Listen for 10–20 minutes right before you go in to take the test.

   b. Listen for 10–20 minutes on your way to school, especially if the test is in the morning.

   c. Listen for 10–20 minutes at lunch if your test is in the afternoon.

continued next page . . .

Show Me

Well, you have to admit it, dear skeptic (which, by the way, is a good thing to be, as all the best scientists and researchers have to be skeptical to ensure an objective and unbiased viewpoint): This section has provided you with scientific proof that music—the right kind of music, used purposefully and skillfully, increases your learning capacity profoundly, while it puts back the fun and the joy of learning at the same time.

So, pull out all of the *From Learning to Doing* activations from each of the five sections you've now read and . . . *Let's Go!!*

Let's Go . . . continued . . .

After the test, reflect on how you felt, how you may have been less stressed, less nervous, more focused, and more alert.

Resources and References

For information on the Mozart recording *Classical Harmonies* and other recordings in the ***Relax with the Classics*** series:

LIND Institute
P.O. Box 14487, San Francisco, CA 94114
1-800-LEARN-R-US (1-800-532-7678)
From overseas: 415-864-3396
FAX: 415-864-1742, E-Mail: lind@lind-institute.com
Visit our web site at: www.lind-institute.com

See page 93 for information about these educational products.

To learn more about Mozart:

Davenport, M. *Mozart.* New York: Avon Books, 1979.

To obtain a copy of the Mozart Effect studies, contact:

Center for the Neurobiology of Learning and Memory
University of California
Irvine, CA 92717
949-824-5193

For information on mind mapping and other fun learning strategies, contact:

Zephyr Press
P.O. Box 66006
Tucson, AZ 85728-6006
1-800-232-2187

Particularly valuable books on mind mapping that Zephyr Press offers:

Mapping Inner Space and *Map It!,* both by Nancy Margulies

Other References:

Boettcher, W. S., Hahn, S. S., Shaw, G. L. "Mathematics and Music: A Search for Insight into Higher Brain Function." *Leonardo Music Journal, vol. 4,* 53–59, 1994.

Campbell, D. *The Mozart Effect.* New York: Avon Books, 1997 (also available through Zephyr Press).

Rauscher, F. H., Shaw, G. L., Ky, K. N. "Listening to Mozart Enhances Spatial Temporal Reasoning: Towards a Neurophysical Basis." *Neuroscience Letters, Letter 185,* 1995, 44–47.

Prokhorov, V. "Will Piano Lessons Make My Child Smarter?" *Parade Magazine,* June 14, 1998, 13–17.

"No one can make you feel inferior without your permission."

– Eleanor Roosevelt (1884–1962)

Design Your Own Study Model

Time to Put It All Together

Remember "way back" in *Section 1* when we asked you to begin thinking about a subject you are now studying that is challenging to you? Remember when we asked you to start looking for ways to use the information in ***Learn with the Classics*** to improve your understanding and your performance in that subject? Well, now it's time to put all of these techniques and tools to good use as you combine all of them to develop your own study model.

Components of the Model

In the next few pages, we recap the *Learning Strategies,* the *Study Tips,* and the highlights of the *From Learning to Doing* activations.

Commitment and Consistency Lead to Success

As you get ready to apply these techniques to your subject, remember that your commitment to using these tools with consistency will enable you to:

- Gain control of your learning.
- Feel confident and relaxed.
- Harness your brain's incredible capacities for learning.
- Enjoy learning—even material that is challenging.

Attitudes That Lead to Success

Remember, this is your first effort at using this kind of study model, so be sure to:

- Be patient with yourself.
- Be creative; take risks. That's how we all learn the best.

- Stay with the program. Look at frustrations as challenges and failures as opportunities to grow and learn. After all, a setback is a setup for a comeback!

- Use the music to relax you and to de-stress.

- Keep your sense of humor. (Mozart had a great one.)

- Trust your own uniqueness and creativity.

Tell Us What You Think

After you've used your study model for a while, please give us your feedback. We'd appreciate it if you would fill out the questionnaire on p. 95 and send it back to us. We'll learn from your experiences, and you'll be a pioneer in this wonderful, fast-growing field. We look forward to hearing from you as you ***Learn with the Classics***.

From Learning to Doing Activations

Section 1

1. Select music that is 55–70 beats per minute and that has the other characteristics mentioned in this section, and play it as you study. Experiment with lowering and raising the volume, basing your choice on the brain wave state—alpha or beta—that you want to enter at a given time.

2. Take short reflection breaks (under 5 minutes) after every 15 minutes of studying and longer breaks (10 to 15 minutes) after every 45 minutes of studying. If necessary, adjust the timing of breaks to suit your own needs and preferences.

3. Use reflection breaks to shift between factual and creative thinking. Notice the feeling of calmness after listening to the music. Pay attention to your new ideas and insights. Use them in the creative portions of your work (such as writing activities and essay tests).

4. Be aware when you are connecting new information with something you already know. Make a mental note of the connections you're making, or write them down.

Section 2

Write your own questions in the margins of your books. (Of course, if the books belong to the school, use Post-its.)

Section 3

1. When you can't remember information that you have already studied, probe your subconscious. Make a list of categories within your subject that you have already studied and that you think you once knew (names of characters in a play, historical dates, mathematical theorems or axioms, the molecular structure of carbon compounds, for example). Have a friend read the list back to you or read it yourself. Relax and listen to the slow Baroque music. See what answers come up to your conscious mind. The more times you do this, the more information will come back to you.

2. Use the systematic reviewing process outlined in this section: Immediately after having read for 45 minutes, take a 10-minute break and then review the material for 5 minutes. After one day, review the material again for 5 minutes. Continue the process until you have completed the entire reviewing process. Then, look back and see how far you've come in your ability to remember information.

Section 4

1. When your mood is low, tell yourself to "clear the deck!" Empty your mind of negative thoughts and self-defeating internal dialogue. Call upon the calming image you have developed (beach or meadow, for example) to help clear your mind. Repeat the word "one" over and over to stop repetitive thinking. Use this exercise whenever negativity prevents you from learning at your best.

2. Use the music regularly and systematically as a prelude (introduction), as a support (foundation), and as a finale (closing) in your studying.

Section 5

1. Listen to the Mozart section of ***Learn with the Classics, The Recording,*** for 10 minutes before each study session.

2. Listen to the Mozart section of the recording before each of your tests. Do this in any or all of the following ways that are possible:

   a. Listen for 10–20 minutes right before you go in to take the test.

   b. Listen for 10–20 minutes on your way to school, especially if the test is in the morning.

   c. Listen for 10–20 minutes at lunch if your test is in the afternoon.

Learning Strategies

Section 1 ❖ Learning Strategy **1**

Select music with the characteristics needed to power up your studying.

55–70-beats-per-minute Baroque music slows down your pulse to mirror the beat of the music; it focuses you; and it makes you more alert and ready to learn.

❖ Learning Strategy **2**

Reflect on what you've learned after each studying session.

This means relaxing completely and letting your brain and the music do the work for you.

❖ Learning Strategy **3**

Shift between alpha and beta brain wave states at will.

As you become familiar with using the music, you will become skilled at shifting states depending upon what kind of thinking you want to engage in at the time—factual or creative.

Section 2 ❖ Learning Strategy **4**

Write your own questions in the textbook margins.

You gain complete control of your material by using your own organizational skills and your own instincts each step along the way.

❖ Learning Strategy **5**

Construct a physical model to learn complex or theoretical material.

When you feel baffled by material or can't get a handle on it, make it physical, make it a "toy."

Section 3 ❖ Learning Strategy **6**

Use music to tap into both sides of the brain at the same time.

Whole brain learning is easier, more fun, and far more effective than right- or left-brain learning alone.

❖ Learning Strategy **7**

Review important newly learned material in a systematic way over the course of six months.

It takes a total of only 20 minutes of review over the course of six months to ensure maximum information transfer from short-term to long-term memory.

Section 4 ❖ Learning Strategy **8**

Use music to focus completely on your learning activity.

You "block out" any extraneous thoughts and emotions and engage totally with what you're doing.

❖ Learning Strategy **9**

Make a game or a sport out of learning experiences.

Just as the challenges in games and sports are fun to surmount, so are the challenges in learning.

❖ Learning Strategy **10**

Use music step by step as you study—as a prelude, a foundation, and a finale.

Used systematically, music supports you in each phase of learning: to focus you, to keep you in optimal study mode, and to integrate what you've learned with what you already know.

Section 5 ❖ Learning Strategy **11**

Use Mozart to boost IQ before taking tests, to prepare for classes that require spatial intelligence, to engage the right brain before attending left-brain–oriented classes, and while reading left-brain–oriented material.

Although the slow Baroque music is wonderful for most studying and learning activities, by adding Mozart to your toolbox of musical learning utensils, you'll get the extra added brain stimulus that Mozart's music in particular offers.

❖ Learning Strategy **12**

Play Mozart to exercise and develop your brain. Once in a while, play this music for no other reason than to feed your brain.

For the sheer joy and benefit of feeding your brain, simply listen to Mozart on a regular basis. Let your brain do the work while you relax, hang out, fool around on the computer, or whatever you do for relaxation and recreation.

Study Tips

Section 1

Take a reflection break about every 15 minutes to contemplate what you've been studying and to allow the information to enter your long-term memory. Keep the music playing. Turn it up a bit so you can hear it a little better.

Section 2

Playing *Jeopardy* Makes Studying a Snap: Write Your Own Questions and You'll Know the Answers.

A major university study revealed that a very simple, efficient, and time-saving study technique is an almost foolproof way to pass tests! Just as in the popular and fun game show *Jeopardy* (in which the contestants come up with the questions to the answers they're given), coming up with your own questions will ultimately give you the right answers.

The technique is simple: When initially reading your material, whenever you come to a specific piece of information, write a question in the margin so that the answer to the question is that piece of information. (If the textbook belongs to the school, don't write in the book. Use Post-its and place them in the margins.) Do this consistently as you go through the text. It's important to do it every time you come to a fact or a series of facts that the author is stressing.

When you review for your test, go back and read your questions. Whenever you can answer a question, great! Just keep on going. You obviously know the answer. When you come to a question that you cannot answer, reread only the portion of text that has the answer. Once you can answer all of your own questions, you have studied sufficiently. You'll be amazed at how much you already know, so that there is no need to reread a great deal of the material. This way, you can efficiently focus your studying only on what you still need to learn.

Here's the kicker: The study showed that 70% of the questions asked in tests are the same questions that you have come up with, so on average, you will have already passed 70% of the test before you take it!

The next time you're unsure of how to tackle a challenging concept or a hard-to-grasp idea, literally separate it into its component parts, represented by the blocks in a LEGO or Tinker Toys set. Form a physical model of connected parts that represent the concept. You can paint the blocks different colors with tempera or acrylic paint or with colored marking pens. Each color can represent the component parts of one category within the whole structure. You can also write on the blocks to indicate what each piece represents. You could mark them with colored paper or masking tape or little doodads—jewelry, paper clips, pieces of colored paper to illustrate specific details of the concept.

(You may think of this as extra "work" for you or as a game you have no time to play, but the more you play physically with information, the deeper it gets imbedded in your long-term memory.)

This is nothing new to you. Remember, you did this when you were a kid. Well, do it again. It still works. Trust your imagination, and it will serve you well. Remember though: Play at it. Have fun with it. If you aren't playing, you're not doing it right. That's the tip: Have fun with it.

Section 3

Develop a systematic reviewing technique over the course of six months whenever you learn significant new information.

Each time you study new material that is important to your subject and that you want to commit to long-term memory, use this review schedule: After studying material for approximately 45 minutes, take a 10-minute break and then review the material for 5 minutes. After one day, review the material for 5 minutes. After one week, review it for 3 minutes. After one month, review it for 3 minutes. After six months, review it for 3 minutes.

Section 4

As you study, it's important to take regular breaks. This gives the brain a breather. The brain enjoys short breaks every 15 minutes and a longer break every 45 minutes. By taking frequent breaks, you allow the brain to relax. This increases its performance. You will also benefit from getting more oxygen to your brain during your breaks. Oxygen is carried through your blood to your brain, so your brain would love it if you got out of your chair and stretched a bit. It's useful to step outside, take some deep breaths of fresh air. This will quickly rush a fresh supply of oxygen to your brain.

Remember: When taking study breaks, you might try turning the music up a little louder. Reflect a bit on what you've been studying, and focus on your breathing. It might inspire you during some breaks to listen to some different music, some of your favorites that always make you feel good and uplifted and will take your mind off your studying for a little while.

Section 5

To prime your brain's spatial intelligence, listen to Mozart before going to math and science classes and to lecture classes. On the ***Learn with the Classics*** recording, the Mozart pieces are cuts 12 to 15. Play Mozart in the background when preparing for a lecture class or when reading complex or deadly dull material.

"Through music, a child
enters a world of beauty,
expresses his inmost self,
tastes the joy of creating,
widens his sympathies,
develops his mind, soothes
and refines his spirit, and
adds grace to his body."

– U.S. Child Welfare Association

LIND's Effective and Easy 4-Part Fitness Program for the Brain

1. **Slow Baroque** for studying, reflecting, activating newly learned information, and relaxing

2. **Mozart** for brainstorming, reading, listening to before tests and before math and science classes and lectures, and for pure brain exercising

3. **Quick Baroque** for brainstorming, energy boosts, kinesthetic learning, and physical exercise

4. **Nineteenth- and twentieth-century romantic and impressionistic** pieces for relaxing, inducing imagination and creativity, evoking imagery, creative writing, and for quiet reflection

Relax with the Classics recordings for each component of the brain-fitness program:

1. **Slow Baroque**—*Largo, Adagio, Pastorale, Andante, Classical Melodies*
2. **Mozart**—*Classical Harmonies*
3. **Quick Baroque**—*Classical Rhythms*
4. **Nineteenth- and twentieth-century romantic and impressionistic**—*Classical Impressions, Interlude, Pianissimo*

Education Products Available from the LIND Institute

RELAX WITH THE CLASSICS®

Beautiful Music That's Good for You™

Baroque and classical masterpieces scientifically chosen and sequenced for optimal learning, teaching, and training; and for relaxation and stress reduction

Largo
Time: 51:23
Beats per minute: 55–70
Music by: Pachelbel, Albinoni, Vivaldi, Mozart, Handel, Gluck, Scarlatti, Caudioso, and others
Order Numbers: CD: L501CD; Tape: L501TA

Adagio
Time: 52:16
Beats per minute: 55–70
Music by: Vivaldi, Mozart, Albinoni, Salieri, Corelli, Michael Haydn, Telemann, Gluck, and Scarlatti
Order Numbers: CD: L502CD; Tape: L502TA

Pastorale
Time: 50:35
Beats per minute: 55–70
Music by: Corelli, J. S. Bach, Galuppi, Gluck, Vivaldi, Albinoni, and Zipoli
Order Numbers: CD: L503CD; Tape: L503TA

Andante
Time: 53:03
Beats per minute: 55–70
Music by: Manfredini, Giuliani, Tartini, Durante, Pergolesi, Handel, Paisiello, Albinoni, and others
Order Numbers: CD: L504CD; Tape: L504TA

Classical Melodies
Time: 59:42
Beats per minute: 55–70
Music by: Handel, Carl Stamitz, Vivaldi, Telemann, and others
Order Numbers: CD: L505CD; Tape: L505TA

Purpose of first five recordings: *Slow Baroque is used for studying, reflecting, activating newly learned information, and relaxing. In addition, play slow Baroque for babies and toddlers when they're cranky. It often calms them down.*

Classical Rhythms
Time: 60:14
Beats per minute: 100–140
Music by: Albinoni, J. S. Bach, Corelli, Vivaldi, and others
Order Numbers: CD: L506CD; Tape: L506TA

Purpose: *Quick Baroque is used for brainstorming, energy boosts (especially effective during study breaks or in the late afternoon when energy often flags), kinesthetic learning, and physical exercise.*

***Classical Harmonies** (all Mozart)*
Time: 63:51
Beats per minute: 55–70
Music by: Mozart
Order Numbers: CD: L507CD; Tape: L507TA

Purpose: *Mozart is used for brainstorming, reading, listening to before tests and before math and science classes and lectures, and for pure brain exercising. Also, play Mozart often for infants and toddlers—especially while they're playing—to foster critical early brain development.*

Classical Impressions
Time: 62:25
Beats per minute: 55–70
Music by: Bizet, Fauré, Grieg, Warlock, and others
Order Numbers: CD: L508CD; Tape: L508TA

Purpose: *Nineteenth- and twentieth-century romantic and impressionistic pieces are used for relaxing, inducing imagination and creativity, evoking imagery, creative writing, and for quiet reflection.*

Pianissimo
Time: 64:07
Beats per minute: 55–70
Solo piano music by: J. S. Bach, Ravel, Schubert, Kalinnikov, and others
Order Numbers: CD: L509CD; Tape: L509TA

Purpose: *Melodic piano pieces are used for studying and for study breaks.*

Interlude
Time: 64:48
Beats per minute: 55–70
Music by: Satie, Rachmaninoff, Rodrigo, Chabrier, and others
Order Numbers: CD: L510CD; Tape: L510TA

Purpose: *Tuneful and uplifting late nineteenth- and early twentieth-century pieces are used for study breaks and reflections.*

Health and Wellness Collection (2 CD set)—***Bach for the Morning*** and ***Handel for the Evening***
Music by: J. S. Bach and Handel
Time: 1 hr. 53 min. (total for 2 recordings)
Beats per minute: Bach recording: 50–120; Handel recording: 120–50
Order Numbers: CD: L601CD
Note: Not available in tape

Purpose: *Stress reduction and health and wellness*—Bach for the Morning *is often used to awaken gently, starting very slowly and building gradually in tempo.* Handel for the Evening *is used to wind down at day's end, beginning at a quicker pace and gradually slowing in tempo.*

Classical Spirit
Time: 66:46
Music: Choral music through the ages (twelfth century to twentieth century), from pure and simple plainchants (Gregorian chants) to richly textured choral masterworks
Order Numbers: CD: L511CD; Tape: L511TA

Purpose: *Chants are used for quieting the mind, relaxing the body, supporting meditation, sparking creativity, and uplifting the mood.*

Collection 1: *Largo, Adagio, Pastorale,* and *Andante* can also be ordered together in a boxed set (not in individual cases).
Order Numbers: CDs: L581CD; Tapes: L581TA

Collection 2: *Classical Melodies, Classical Harmonies, Classical Rhythms,* and *Classical Impressions* can also be ordered together in a boxed set (not in individual cases).
Order Numbers: CDs: L582CD; Tapes: L582TA

LEARN WITH THE CLASSICS: Using Music to Study Smart at Any Age
Order Numbers: Book with CD: LB201CD; Book with tape: LB201TA

To order: **1-800-LEARN-R-US** (1-800-532-7678) • From overseas: 415-864-3396
FAX: 415-864-1742 • E-Mail: lind@lind-institute.com
Visit our web site at: www.lind-institute.com

"Having courage doesn't mean you're not afraid of doing something. It means you are *afraid, but you do it anyway."*

– Eleanor Roosevelt (1884–1962)

cut pages from book along this line — then fold according to lines on address page — staple or tape closed — then mail

Tell Us What You Think About *LEARN WITH THE CLASSICS*

Would you like to be on our mailing list? ☐ yes ☐ no

Name ______________________________

Street Address ______________________________

City ____________________ State __________ Zip __________

What ideas have worked best for you? ______________________________

____

____

What ideas have not worked well for you? ______________________________

____

____

What do you think about making music a central element in your learning activities? ____

____

Was anything unclear to you? What was it? ______________________________

____

____

Have your grades improved from using ***Learn with the Classics***? (Or, if you're not concerned with grades—Has your performance improved from using ***Learn with the Classics?***)

____

____

Do you have more confidence in your ability to learn? ________________

In which of the following areas of learning do you think you've improved:

- ☐ More creativity
- ☐ Greater relaxation
- ☐ Reduced stress
- ☐ Increased memory
- ☐ Increased focus
- ☐ More fun
- ☐ Deeper comprehension of challenging material

The things I like best about ***Learn with the Classics***: ________________

____

____

The things I like least about ***Learn with the Classics***: ________________

____

____

How could these problems be solved? ________________

____

What do you think about Baroque and classical music?

- ☐ I like them.
- ☐ I don't like them, but they work for me in learning.

cut pages from book along this line — then fold according to lines on address page — staple or tape closed — then mail

cut pages from book along this line — then fold according to lines on address page — staple or tape closed — then mail

- [ ] I don't like them, and they don't work for me.
- [ ] I don't know.

Do you use the music at other times than just studying? When? ______________________

____

Topics you wish had been in ***Learn with the Classics***: ______________________________

____

Topics you'd like taken out of ***Learn with the Classics***: ____________________________

____

Are there enough activities for you? ____

Are you a:

- [ ] Student
- [ ] Teacher
- [ ] Corporate trainer
- [ ] Other professional
- [ ] Parent
- [ ] Other ____

Tell us about a positive experience you had with ***Learn with the Classics***: _______________

____

____

____

staple here if you are not enclosing this questionnaire in an envelope

fold here

____

____

____

place
stamp
here

LIND Institute
P.O. Box 14487
San Francisco, CA 94114
USA

fold here, and fold this panel under top panel

Any other comments? ____

____

____

____

____

"One ought, every day at least, to hear a little song, read a good poem, see a fine picture, and, if it were possible, to speak a few reasonable words."

– Goethe (1749–1832)

About the Authors

Ole Andersen

Ole Andersen is music publisher and president of the LIND Institute in San Francisco. With his partner, the late Dr. Charles Schmid, he founded the LIND Institute in 1973. Together, they developed a teaching methodology—the LIND Method of Accelerated Learning, Teaching, and Training—which combines Accelerated Learning techniques with the purposeful use of Baroque and classical music in the classroom. Their proprietary music series, ***Relax with the Classics***—designed specifically for use in learning and teaching—is used throughout the world as a key component in advanced teaching and training. Since Schmid's death, Andersen has designed a second series of ***Relax with the Classics*** recordings for learning and teaching and has published the *Health and Wellness Collection* and *Classical Spirit*, a chronology of chants. He continues to design and produce special music programs for specific purposes.

Marcy Marsh

Marcy Marsh is currently a writer and editor, specializing in scholarly publications in higher education. She also writes and consults on education issues for the LIND Institute. She has taught secondary and adult education in both public and private schools, in the United States and France. As a high school English teacher, she experimented extensively with incorporating various media—including music, dance, visual arts, film, and drama—into her teaching and was instrumental in gaining inclusion for these techniques in the school district curriculum. She has developed multimedia curricula for teaching English as a second language to adults and adolescents and has trained other educators on developing creative teaching environments that involve students of all learning styles through the use of diverse media.

Arthur Harvey

Dr. Arthur Harvey has worked extensively throughout the world as a musician and educator. He currently trains and consults on the uses of music in health care and education for the LIND Institute. He designed ***Relax with the Classics'*** *Health and Wellness* collection specifically for use in medical institutions, long-term care facilities, and for individuals interested in using music to improve or maintain health and reduce stress. He teaches at the University of Hawaii and is the current president of the Hawaii Music Educators Association. He has taught music at all levels, including early childhood; special needs; secondary-level humanities; and music appreciation. He has taught college and graduate school courses in music education pedagogy; music and the brain; brain research and learning styles; music theory, form, and analysis; choral arranging; counterpoint; and the psychology of music. He was instrumental in establishing the Program for Arts in Medicine at the University of Louisville's School of Medicine.

LEARN WITH THE CLASSICS, The Recording

This book comes with a companion recording of beautiful, scientifically selected Baroque and classical masterpieces.

1. Johann Sebastian BACH	*Air on G String, Capella Istropolitana/Edlinger*	*5:17*
2. Johann Sebastian BACH	*Largo from Piano Concerto No. 5 in F Minor, Chang, Cassovia, Stankovsky*	*2:46*
3. Georg-Friedrich HANDEL	*Air from Water Music, Capella Istropolitana/Warchal*	*1:57*
4. Georg-Phillip TELEMANN	*Viola Concerto – First Movement, Capella Istropolitana/Edlinger*	*3:42*
5. Georg-Friedrich HANDEL	*Larghetto from Violin Concerto in A Minor, Op. 6, No. 4, Capella Istropolitana/Kopelman*	*2:30*
6. Antonio VIVALDI	*Largo from Violin Concerto in A Minor, Op. 3, No. 6, Pazdera/Accademia Ziliniana*	*2:28*
7. Tomaso ALBINONI	*Adagio from Oboe Concerto in D Minor, Op. 9, No. 2, Camden/The London Virtuosi/Georgiadis*	*5:19*
8. Johann Sebastian BACH	*Largo ma non tanto from Concerto for Two Violins and Strings in D Minor, Nishizaki, Jablokov/Capella Istropolitana/Dohnányi*	*6:46*
9. Georg-Friedrich HANDEL	*Larghetto from Xerxes, Capella Istropolitana/Edlinger*	*3:38*
10. Georg-Friedrich HANDEL	*Oboe Concerto, Capella Istropolitana/Edlinger*	*3:06*
11. Georg-Friedrich HANDEL	*Pastoral Symphony from the Messiah, Capella Istropolitana/Krechek*	*3:05*
12. Wolfgang A. MOZART	*Andante from Piano Concerto No. 21 in C Major, Vienna Mozart Orchestra/Leitner*	*6:14*
13. Wolfgang A. MOZART	*Andante un poco adagio from Piano Concerto No. 6 in B Flat Major, Jandó/Concentus Hungaricus/Antál*	*5:48*
14. Wolfgang A. MOZART	*Adagio from Flute Quartet No. 1 in D Major, Gérard/Ensemble Villa Musica*	*2:42*
15. Wolfgang A. MOZART	*Rondeau from Flute Quartet No. 1 in D Major, Gérard/ Ensemble Villa Musica*	*4:15*
	Total Playing Time	***60:19***

LEARN WITH THE CLASSICS, The Recording, is a sampler of musical selections from the ***RELAX WITH THE CLASSICS***® series.